# Smart Biology

## A New Look at Life

For Lizzy, keep on truckin'.

ISBN: 9798545560783

"Intelligence is based on how efficient a species became at doing the things they need to survive".

Charles Darwin

Life is wetware, and it is time to recognise that organisms are smart. Biology is the study of living computers. The approach is to ask what would be involved in simulating an organism's behaviour with a robot. This provides insight into life's computing and how clever organisms change our view of biology.

We deal with cybernetics, defined by mathematician Norbert Wiener as "control and communication in the animal and the machine". This book extends Wiener's animals to cover all life and its driver – cognition. In Wiener's words, "Two of the phenomena which we consider to be characteristic of living systems are the power to learn and the power to reproduce themselves".

A book about life's intelligence covers several different disciplines. To make it more accessible, I have avoided jargon wherever possible. Using broad stroke heuristics is sensible rather than describing the intricate details that the reader can check with a simple internet search.

Throughout the text, I have put some representative references in the footnotes. The mentions are not complete or exhaustive but are included to help readers follow up on topics. It was possible to describe computer science, cybernetics, and information theory without recourse to equations or explicit mathematics. Similarly, I have grouped together bacteria and archaea for presentational reasons. Well-known abbreviations such as DNA and RNA are used without elaboration. I use the phrase 'different genes' instead of the more accurate allele and make other minor simplifications to make the text easier to read. Such simplification will not trouble a professional scientist. By necessity, I have ignored several forms of implicit censorship.

Some with a tiresome philosophical inclination have been attempting to impose restrictions on the study of life. For example, they urge biologists not to use methods that work well in machine intelligence or robotics. Here we take a more scientific viewpoint and ignore the old-fashioned boundaries from the precomputer era. Arbitrary restrictions are disregarded. People who do not like an iconoclastic approach can always burn the book – I believe that is their classic response.

Commenting on the unfortunate evolution vs religion saga was unavoidable. Sadly, it is not evident that science is an empirical discipline of trial and error with no bearing on religious belief. Throughout the book, I have referred to the idea of selfish genes and Richard Dawkins' popularisation of Neo-Darwinian ideas. This focus was helpful because of the widespread belief in Dawkins' particular and over the top brand of evolutionary philosophy. I don't know Richard Dawkins and obviously intend no personal criticism. However, Dawkins' work provides some wonderfully extreme statements, which help simplify the presentation.

Some will always criticise a book on cognition and life as intelligent design. This criticism is beyond stupid; computing is not religion. However, the *ad hominem* argument is a standard response of some who believe in biology as nature red in tooth and claw. This irrationality brings me to covering psychopathy in the text. Connecting the dots between philosophy and personality has been bypassed in polite society. However, it was necessary to disclose the social background of evolutionary theory over the past 200 years. Episodes like the eugenics movement need a proper explanation if we are to avoid them in the future.

"The major thing is to view biology as an information science".

Leroy Hood

# Contents

"Computers are like humans – they do everything except think".

John von Neumann

# Life is Wetware

"The Encyclopedia Galactica defines a robot as a mechanical apparatus designed to do the work of a man. The marketing division of the Sirius Cybernetics Corporation defines a robot as 'Your plastic pal who's fun to be with'. The Hitchhiker's Guide to the Galaxy defines the marketing division of the Sirius Cybernetic Corporation as 'a bunch of mindless jerks who'll be the first against the wall when the revolution comes'".

Douglas Adams

We need a more intelligent approach to biology. Look carefully, and even the simplest microorganism is intelligent. Living creatures adapt and strive to survive. They move, metabolise, and reproduce, all while adapting to a hostile environment. In this account, we are concerned with the cognition needed for survival, hunting, and avoiding predation, rather than genius or consciousness.

A characteristic of life is the ability to process information. Life computes, and smart organisms make decisions. The evolution of smart organisms is quite different from explanations of natural selection acting on selfish genes. Evolution is a history of cognition.

The purpose of this book is to investigate how biocomputing changes our understanding of life and evolution. Here we use the words "think" and "intelligence" in the modern sense. With the widespread availability of computing and communication devices, such as smartphones, to say a machine "is thinking" is everyday talk. So here, the term smart is used similarly to its use in what has become commonplace technology.

Machine intelligence is widely accepted, as are its limitations. However, it is undeniable that systems made of silicon are capable of advanced computing and a form of artificial intelligence (AI). These devices have transformed human society in a few short decades.

Assuming living creatures can do similar computations has equally dramatic effects on our understanding of life.

## Darwin's Brains

Charles Darwin was being metaphorical when describing the tips of roots as plant brains. In the late 19th century, Darwin was at a loss to describe plant behaviour. He explained that the root tip is sensitive and has the power of directing movement. In other words, it acts like the brain in one of the lower animals. Despite the technological limitations of the time, Darwin was foresighted. He understood that a species evolves the intelligence necessary for doing the things they need to survive.

Darwin merely claimed that the root tips might explain a plant's ability to gather and process information. The words he needed to say what he meant were not yet available. He was popularising some new and unfamiliar ideas. Critically, Darwin worked without knowledge of computers and Alan Turing's explanation of machine intelligence. He could not use the language of computer science, which would arrive in the next century.

Darwin did the best he could and talked about plant root tips as brains, which people at that time accepted as having some potential for thinking. Well, at least philosophers admitted that humans could think. Unfortunately, contemporary scientists too often considered animals little more than automatons, mindless meat robots. Unsurprisingly, these scientists dismissed Darwin's idea. Nothing resembles a brain at the tip of plant roots; they are made of different materials and are microscopically dissimilar. Plants are not animals, they don't have brains, and they don't think.

The idea that plants could think was beyond the pale. Still, Darwin's exceptional biological wisdom led him to describe plant roots acting to accumulate and process data. Nowadays, computer scientists would understand straight away and have no issue with Darwin's impression. Unfortunately, scientists still suffer from the language used to describe intelligence. Philosophers have one meaning of the word that differs from that used by computer scientists. As might be expected, psychologists have several interpretations of what it means to be intelligent. In their turn, engineers have a different attitude.

## Green Beard Effect?

The idea of a gene for green beards illustrates the problem at the heart of biological theory. Following William Hamilton's ideas,[1] Richard Dawkins imagined a sex-linked gene that produced green beards. Hamilton had suggested a gene that gave the ability to recognise others with the same gene. A green beard is distinctive, and thus it is easy to identify people with the gene. Furthermore, the gene enables green beards to help each other and thus help themselves.

Both Dawkins and Hamilton realised that the green beard gene was unlikely to occur. A mutation for the two properties of greenness and helping each other was implausible in the same gene. Hamilton suggested he was considering "something like a supergene". However, many established developments in biology are improbable. We can allow the properties to spread over several linked genes. So the dubiousness of the association is not the issue. Still, look a little more closely at the green beard story, and it falls apart. There is a mechanism for genes producing proteins like the keratin in hair and their properties such as colour. Thus we can accept green beards – it's what genes do. Nonetheless, everything else in the story is nonsense.

Consider what this simple gene is being asked to do. First, the organism needs to know it's a green beard (identify itself) and have a way to recognise others with green beards. Then, it requires an advanced algorithm of some form to preferentially help other green beards. In other words, Hamilton's story starts from the assumption that the organism can process information. In computing terms, it has sensors to gather data, a processor to provide the logic, software to compute the implications, and a decision-making process. Supergene or not, information is fundamental and cannot be ignored.

---

[1] Hamilton W.D. (1964) The genetical evolution of social behaviour, J. Theor. Biol., 7, 17-52.

## Starting Again

We can start again with the idea of smart organisms and come to some startling conclusions. Firstly, evolution is misunderstood since living organisms are autonomous and generate their own behaviour. This new approach does not involve a big conceptual step from current thinking, but the results are profound.

The systems theorist Ross Ashby argued that a "dynamic system generates its own form of intelligent life and is self-organising". Moreover, "every isolated determinate dynamic system obeying unchanging laws will develop 'organisms' that are adapted to their 'environments'". As we shall see

Evolution generates smart organisms.

Similarly, Alan Turing explained more about biology than many people appreciate, and his ideas are consistent with Darwin's theory. Notably, Turing considered the question "can machines think" meaningless and not worthy of discussion. Science works by getting a question and testing it by experiment. So Turing started with the question, is a thinking machine possible? To answer this question, Turing suggested building an artificially intelligent machine and comparing its output with an example of thinking (whatever that is). Naturally, some philosophers challenge this approach, but their alternative ideas are commonly unscientific – not testable by experiment.

In Alan Turing's time, people thought to be a good chess player required high intelligence. It takes a gifted human and years of practice to achieve grandmaster standard. Nowadays, many have tried playing chess with a good software game. The result can be disheartening for all but the most skilled humans who have trained well. It is also humbling to realise that people regarded chess as a demanding intellectual exercise before computers started beating them.

Machines can play chess and play well. As a result, many no longer consider chess to require real intelligence. Instead, they simply moved the goalposts. The claim is that if a machine can do it, it does not take real intelligence. A chess-playing machine is thus not intelligent, even if it can beat the person making the claim. By this way of thinking, the definition of intelligence is something a machine cannot do. The response has a name, the AI Effect – or whatever a machine can do, the answer is "that's not thinking".[2]

Here, like Turing, we are only concerned with science. The critical question is can a creature influence its survival and reproduction by gathering and processing information. The answer to this question is a clear yes. Evolution depends on behaviour. Scientists still have difficulty defining what life is, but we know it when we see it.

A mushroom is alive while the adjacent rock is not. The characteristics we use to identify living things are telling. The inert rock just sits there. A living mushroom has structure, movement, shape, growth, and interacts with its surroundings. The mushroom is shapely, symmetrical, uses energy, and appears overnight in a crowd of near-identical copies. While the mushroom exhibits behaviour, the rock still just sits there.

As their name exemplifies, organisms are systems in which genes are a component. Cells store digital information in genes, but there is a lot more to life than DNA. Isolate DNA in a test tube, and it is just goop. DNA is inert chemical data that needs a cell to decode it. Genes store and control the code for making proteins. Some biologists suggest genes are the central component of life itself and the basic unit of biological information.[3] As we shall see, they are not. Others claim that natural selection acting on genes can explain life.[4] Once again, we shall recognise that it cannot. A few biotechnologists assume that humans can control evolution by manipulating genes. Well, only to a trivial but dangerous extent.

A cell is to DNA what a computer is to a hard drive. Biocomputing is more than just genes. Take the ubiquitous and essential cell membrane that has existed throughout life on earth. This double-layered arrangement is composed of ordered phospholipid molecules covering cells and forming a barrier to the outside world. Membranes pack together inside cells, helping form the structure and separating compartments. Notably, the cell

---

[2] McCorduck P. (2004) Machines Who Think, CRC Press.
[3] Mukherjee S. (2017) The Gene: An Intimate History, Vintage.
[4] Dawkins R. (2016) The Selfish Gene: 40th Anniversary edition, Oxford Univ. Press.

membrane generates itself; it is self-organising. Rather like bubbles in soapy water, double-layered membranes form spontaneously from their constituent molecules. No genetic instructions are necessary. Many of a cell's components are similarly self-organising.[5] Far from being a new-age idea, self-organisation and emergence are basic features of modern physics and chemistry.

Every part of an organism's life needs information, from growth and development to fitness to survive and reproduce. An organism's behaviour necessary for survival is relatively straightforward. We can describe it using ideas from computer science and robotics and find that

Smart organisms have a survival advantage.

Usually, scientists describe living things by their use of energy, growth, and reproduction. However, information is equally fundamental and generally ignored. Living things depend on organisation, control, and information processing. At the time of writing, engineers attempting to simulate a living organism have only limited success, as with the Boston Dynamics robot dog Spot.[6] Engineers built Spot of metal and plastic; he moves awkwardly and appears mechanical. However, there is no reason why a convincing simulation of an animal is impossible. Androids are a staple in science fiction, and early robot companions[7] and sexbots with rudimentary AI exist.

Creatures like Spot are used to investigate robotics and artificial intelligence. Simulating a dog with an autonomous machine provides a device potentially useful for dangerous environments. For example, it might have applications in high radiation areas of nuclear power stations. Unfortunately, the danger is that Spot will mature as a terminator dog. We live in a world developing drones, artificial killer insects, and exploding fish — more ways of killing each other. Sadly, the first autonomous robots have recently been deployed and killed

[5] Karsenti E. (2008) Self-organization in cell biology, Nat. Rev. Mol. Cell Biol., 9, 255–262.
[6] Spot the robot dog, Bostondynamics.com, accessed Jan. 2021.
[7] Bradwell H.L. *et al* (2019) Companion robots for older people: importance of user-centred design demonstrated through observations and focus groups comparing preferences of older people and roboticists in South West England, BMJ Open, e032468.

people in a Middle East conflict. Still, Spot can give a superficial impression of a real animal's behaviour.

We don't need to resurrect the old ideas of a clockwork universe or vitalism. The idea is to find out how closely machines can simulate the behaviour of living organisms. But, of course, there are limits to the engineering approach. Part of the scientist's role is to break down life's processes into simple mechanical and molecular descriptions. Nevertheless, good scientists understand there are limits to such reductionism.

## Emergence

The brain's dominant scientific model is a biological computer, but this is an imperfect analogy. Knowledge of synaptic transmission or the anatomy of nerve cells does little to explain human creativity and behaviour. On the other hand, learning more about the brain's internal workings does not obscure the mystery of its fantastic holistic function. Emergence is not the ideal term for what is happening, but it is widespread in computing and physics.

It is difficult to account for emergence by reducing a system to its components. Nonetheless, simple chemistry shows how successful reductionism can be. Sodium is a violently reactive metal that spontaneously and aggressively oxidises in water or even damp air. The military used chlorine as a lung destroying poison gas, most notably in World War One. Adding these two reactive chemicals produces plain old common salt. Physicists can explain how this combination of gas and metal generates salt and even predict the crystal structure using quantum mechanics. Still, not everything is so straightforward.

Snowflakes form when ice crystals spontaneously generate fantastic symmetrical patterns. As children learn in school, water is the combination of two gasses, oxygen and hydrogen. It is relatively easy to predict a molecular structure for water from the nature of the individual atoms. Here things go a little awry. Scientists don't really understand water, which is a strange substance with odd properties.[8] It is found as a solid, a liquid, and a gas under normal conditions.

---

[8] Ball P. (2008) Water: water—an enduring mystery, Nature, 452(7185), 291-292.

Unusually, it expands when it freezes, making ice float. Ice typically has a hexagonal structure but forms cubic crystals in the atmosphere.[9] There are 17 reported forms of ice crystal, and several more may occur.[10] Even the liquid water that is so familiar has unique properties and may exist in two or more forms.[11] Moreover, the mystery of the snowflake is not alone.

Like water, that other substance at the heart of life, carbon has many surprises. For example, it forms diamonds at high pressures deep within the earth. Diamond is, of course, that hard crystalline substance used in engagement rings. At lower pressures, carbon forms graphite, the "lead" in pencils. Graphite is comprised of hexagonal molecular sheets piled together. Diamond and graphite are the common types of carbon we know from everyday life. Still, scientists now think that carbon may exist in hundreds of different forms.[12]

Buckyballs are football like molecules of carbon that scientists named Buckminster fullerenes after the famous inventor. The buckyball discovery gained the 1996 Nobel Prize in Chemistry. Other fullerenes include graphite-like molecular sheets rolled into carbon nanotubes. Another Nobel Prize was awarded in 2010 for work on single molecular sheets of carbon isolated from graphite. Once discovered, scientists found fullerenes were widespread; they even occur in candle smoke.

Familiar and apparently simple substances hold surprises not predicted in advance. Swarms of molecules or organisms have properties that were not expected from their components. We will later see how swarm intelligence is an emergent property of crowds of objects following the simplest rules. As Alan Turing demonstrated, the output of such systems is not necessarily predictable.[13]

---

[9] Murray B.J. *et al* (2005) The formation of cubic ice under conditions relevant to Earth's atmosphere, Nature, 434(7030), 202-205.

[10] Salzmann C.G. (2019) Advances in the experimental exploration of water's phase diagram, J. Chem. Phys., 150(6), 060901.

[11] Maestro L.M. *et al* (2016) On the existence of two states in liquid water: impact on biological and nanoscopic systems, Int. J. of Nanotech., 13 (8–9), 667–677.

[12] Hoffmann R. *et al* (2016) Homo Citans and Carbon Allotropes: For an Ethics of Citation, Angew. Chem. Int. Ed. Engl., 55(37), 10962–10976.

[13] Classic example: the Halting problem, or determining, whether an arbitrary computer program will finish running, or continue forever.

*Intelligent systems are not always predictable.*

Some people are full of hubris about how their intelligence and technology put them above other animals. Homo sapiens have been around for 100,000 years or so. This period seems long, but amoebae have survived in harmony with the environment for hundreds of millions of years. By contrast, human progress and the population explosion rest on extravagant energy use, which is increasingly difficult to source. In addition, humans have been expending prodigious effort on war, destruction of their environment, and a massive biodiversity reduction.

Several challenges threaten the continued existence of the human species. However, instead of searching for solutions, people work on short-term financial and other trivial advantages. So it is not even clear that humans will last out the current century. In evolutionary terms, humans may be a short-lived species that were too dumb to deal with some fundamental problems that numerous other organisms have solved.

## Brains

Humans are brain centred about thinking. Some anthropologists claimed Homo sapiens evolved a giant brain that separated us from the rest of the animal kingdom, including our nearest ape relatives. However, Neanderthal brains may have been larger.[14] Sperm whales, elephants, and dolphins have substantially bigger brains than people do. A standard response is human brains may be smaller but have more neurons and connections. So the current special pleading is that humans are superior because they have higher quality brains. Still, a biochemist might respond that all mammal brains contain remarkably similar stuff.

*Brains are merely one approach to cognition.*

In reality, brains are overrated. When considering how animals might process information, the first stop is often the brain and nervous system. That is a familiar idea. However, biological computing occurs in every cell down to the molecular level. For

---

[14] Ponce de León M.S. *et al* (2008) Neanderthal brain size at birth provides insights into the evolution of human life history, PNAS, 105(37), 13764-13768.

example, cells use genes for storing information using a genetic code that is logically equivalent to the bits, zeros and ones, in a computer file.

Like Darwin's critics, many people assume it is obvious that plants can't think, as they do not have a brain. Once again, this idea is confused. Without a brain, computers translate text from Chinese to English and run the stock market. People now accept that an inanimate machine can demonstrate impressive information processing capacity. In that case, there is no point in dismissing a plant's computing ability because it does not have a nervous system.

Some people find it uncomfortable to discuss plant intelligence. I suggest they might overcome this feeling by looking down a microscope at some pond water. Tiny single-celled creatures are moving about and interacting. Their activities are often quick and seemingly random. Thermal jiggling batters the little critters around, but their actions are not merely random Brownian motion. As we shall see, microorganisms, and single cells in general, are crammed full of computing gear. Taking the time to look makes it apparent.

Microorganisms need to be able to control movement, sense their environment, and act appropriately. They seem purposeful. Some are hunting, searching out prey while avoiding being eaten themselves. A paramecium has to identify microorganisms it can eat from an amoeba that might eat it. Reproduction requires decision-making. The paramecium may divide, splitting to make two offspring, keep hunting, or move off to new pastures to find a more comfortable temperature and abundant food. A little thought indicates that the microorganisms have similar computing demands to large animals.

Even the simplest microorganism can be smart. Microorganism behaviour was brought home to me when I saw a report about *Le Blob*, a slime mould called Physarum polycephalum, finding the correct path through a maze.[15] A slime mould achieving this result was surprising. Solving a maze is often a problem in puzzle books intended for intelligent adults. Fortunately, there was an explanation for the behaviour.

_____

[15] Nakagaki T. *et al* (2000) Maze-solving by an amoeboid organism, Nature, 407, 470.

*Le Blob* was spreading out, sending out feelers if you like through the maze. It reinforced the paths where it found food and drew back from places where it found nothing. Simple. Physarum was physically constructing what computer scientists call a decision tree with its body. With Len Noriega, I modelled the process by applying an artificial intelligence algorithm derived from ants searching out food in their local environment.[16] In other words, the lowly Physarum was using intelligent methods, which occur in many other animal species. How *Le Blob* does this calculation remains to be fully worked out. However, the effect is the same. A simple slime mould can process information and act in a way that we can reasonably describe as smart.

Biologists often bypass the diverse behaviours of single cells, preferring to focus on other matters. While writing this, I am at home locked down by the government response to a virus. People forget that the antibody and cell immunity protecting people from disease depends on cellular processing. Antibodies are a biological approach to pattern recognition, one of the more advanced forms of computing. Indeed, artificial immune systems provide a method for machine intelligence.[17] So it is difficult to argue convincingly that cellular biocomputing is unimportant when modern medicine and cutting-edge machine intelligence systems copy it.

Scientists base much of modern biology on the living organism as a machine, including bioengineering and molecular biology. However, a living organism is more than a simple device; it self-replicates and reproduces itself. The complexity leads to two opposite views to the science of life. For many, reductionism and competition contrasts with the more holistic Gaia style approach that emphasises cooperation and synergy.[18] Nevertheless, biology is quite a different ball game when you start from the premise that the beasties are smart. Competition and cooperation are just optional strategies that do not define evolution.

---

[16] Hickey S. Noriega L. (2008) Relationship between structure and information processing in Physarum polycephalum, Inter. J. Modelling, Identification and Control, 4(4), 348-356.
[17] Dasgupta D. *et al* (2003) Artificial immune system (AIS) research in the last five years, The Congress on Evolutionary Computation, Canberra, ACT, Australia.
[18] Lovelock J. (2016) Gaia: A New Look at Life on Earth, Oxford Univ. Press.

## Censorship

Science is an inductive practical process based on ideas tested by experiments. So it does not matter if a hypothesis offends a philosopher; all that matters is that scientists can test it.

*Science is iconoclastic.*

For some reason, scientists have allowed philosophers and others to place arbitrary restrictions on biology. Suggest your pet dog is hungry or happy, and they accuse you of anthropomorphism. You are projecting human traits onto a dumb animal. This thought crime is supposed to indicate a lack of objectivity. To dog owners and many scientists, the claim is absurd.

A dog may be communicating that it will engage in rapid eating if fed. Dog owners can test this observation with the offer of food, which the animal may gulp down or reject. The dog owner's "hungry" is shorthand for a longer and more acceptable description. "My observation of the animal indicates that it is communicating that it will immediately engage in rapid eating behaviour if food is available". I'm not sure this version is more accurate or conveys more information than the single word "hungry".

The philosophers making such demands seem to have forgotten that the idea of anthropomorphism depends on a distinction between humans and other animals. Say a person is hungry, and there is no issue. Still, a person and a dog are both mammals with similar physiology. Both can be hungry and can weaken or die without food. It is not the human language that makes the difference because the person might be dumb or from foreign parts. Anthropomorphism depends on humans being extraordinary and unique animals.

## The Purpose

The purpose of this book is to provide new insights into life and its evolution. However, many philosophers believe only humans can have a purpose. Therefore, they urge biologists to remove the idea from their descriptions of reality.

Once again, humans are supposed to be unique special animals. They alone can act purposefully have an aim or intent. Only people act intentionally because only humans are intelligent. This claim fails when compared with direct observation of life. Let's put purpose into context. Organisms act for self-preservation. Evolution rewards any animal with behaviour that makes it more likely to survive. The result is the survival instinct, or the urge to live.

Similarly, the sexual instinct leads to an animal engaging in reproductive behaviour. Any species that does not increase its chance of survival and reproduction is likely to become extinct. Animals are goal-oriented; they aim to eat, live, and leave offspring.

Survival and reproduction are goal-oriented.

The idea of purpose in biology has a long history going back to Greek philosophy. But the postmodern view is that biologists should avoid explanations based on intent. You might say your trip to the shops was because you wanted to buy some chocolate. However, your dog does not have a purpose when bringing her lead to you and pulling you to the front door. We are back to hubris, where animals are lower organisms, incapable of intelligent thought. Animals only behave according to some pre-programmed instinct.

Biologists talk about purpose all the time. Richard Dawkins is an extreme example of a famous biologist who demands an absence of purpose but then popularises the vague idea that genes are selfish. One way biologists get around the paradox is to discuss apparent purpose or teleonomy. We are to accept that animals only seem to be goal-directed. It is an artefact of them being adapted to their way of life by evolution.

By contrast, it is straightforward to build a computer or robot that can learn to act purposefully. What is more, there is no measurable difference in behaviour between real or apparent purpose. So a biologist is free of this philosophical censorship as it isn't testable by experiment.

Ask a physiologist the purpose of the heart, and he will probably reply to pump blood. It's what the heart does. Pumping blood is necessary for continuing life. However, allowing a purpose is supposed to bring in god and teleology, an overall aim to life. The management scientist Stafford Beer might have asked the philosophers how many angels can cabriole on the head of a pin. As Beer put it, "The purpose of a system is what it does. There is after all no point in claiming that the purpose of a system is to do what it constantly fails to do". In other words, the heart pumps blood.

Beer started in operations research in the British war office and later used a systems approach to business decision-making. He had no problem with purpose defining it using POSIWID, or

The purpose of a system is what it does.

In Beer's words: "This is a basic dictum. It stands for a bald fact, which makes a better starting point in seeking understanding than … good intention, prejudices about expectations, moral judgment, or sheer ignorance of circumstances". In this way, the purpose of something is not the designer's intention; it is just a property of the system.

A popular explanation of POSIWID might be, ignore what they say and watch what they do. When a politician says he gives humanitarian aid to help an underdeveloped country, look at the outcome. The result may be the enrichment of the country's president, the benefit of organised charities, and contracts to extract resources. The name they give to the handout is irrelevant. There may be nothing humanitarian about it. Similarly, when a central bank prints additional currency, it preferentially benefits the government and financiers who receive the funds first.[19] There is no need to invoke conspiracy theories. However described, it is what it is.

By employing purpose sensibly, we can return biology to its base of direct observation and measurement. For example, describing a hawk hunting a shrew as aiming to eat and provide its family with the energy needed to survive is sound science and engineering.

An organism's evolutionary purpose is to survive and reproduce.

## Darwin's Intelligence

A quaint idea dominates Darwin's Origin of Species. It begins with the human selection of varieties of animal and plant breeds. People have been breeding varieties for centuries, leading to dogs as different as a Chihuahua and the Great Dane. Darwin describes this

---

[19] The Cantillon effect.

as artificial selection. In artificial selection, an outside human intelligence directed the choice and controlled the breeding pairs.

Natural selection was the same process but occurred without the intervention of intelligence. The difference is philosophical rather than scientific. Once again, separating artificial from natural selection can imply that humans are the only organisms with intelligence.

What if we trained a computer to select dogs for breeding? I don't mean programmed but trained as in teaching a neural network computer. Let it loose to generate a new canine variety using its own aesthetic criteria as a guide. We now have machine selection in addition to natural and artificial (human) selection. It turns out that scientists are investigating neural networks to improve plant breeding, particularly by using them as a decision aid.[20] Decisions are no longer the unique domain of people; human decision-making cannot match machines in many applications.

The difference between the domestication of animals and natural selection is not clear-cut. Animals can choose their mates. Moreover, how animals process data is not different in principle from those of an electronic computer or even a person. Some of the confusion comes from the 17th-century mathematician Rene Descartes. Descartes is perhaps best known for his *cogito ergo sum* philosophy, or I think therefore I am. Long before the invention of the computer, Descartes thought the brain was a kind of machine. He suggested that mathematics could explain the operation of the human mind.

Descartes also believed that humans were unique, and animals were simple machines without any capacity for thinking or actual suffering. Unsurprisingly, antivivisectionists blame these ideas for the misuse of animals. Moreover, Darwin's view of animals could be equally humane, "There is no fundamental difference between man and the higher mammals in their mental faculties".

---

[20] Eg: Rad. M.R.N. (2018) Artificial neural networks and its role in plant breeding under drought stress, CIACR, 1(2), 33-35; Silva G.N. *et al* (2014) Neural networks for predicting breeding values and genetic gains, Scientia Agricola, 71(6), 494-498.

"Teleology is like a mistress to a biologist: he cannot live without her but he's unwilling to be seen with her in public".

J.B.S. Haldane

# Turing Is As Turing Does

"If it looks like a duck, and quacks like a duck, we have at least to consider the possibility that we have a small aquatic bird of the family anatidae on our hands".

Douglas Adams

The father of the computer Alan Turing had a disregard for convention. Despite being a world-leading academic, he would keep his trousers up with string. In the war, he rode an old broken-down woman's bike despite the social norms of the time. Supremely practical, he rode wearing a gas mask as he suffered from hay fever. The bicycle chain would keep slipping off the cogs. Still, Turing worked out a way he could keep the chain on. He rode successfully by counting the pedal turns and reversing his pedalling at intervals. Asked about the state of his bike, he would point and ask, "Who's going to pinch that?"

His rejection of social rules reflected the essential way he thought about science. Turing would ignore the established ideas and set off on his own from first principles. His intellectual bravery put him way ahead of his contemporaries.

Alan Turing has received belated fame for his work in Bletchley Park and for helping break the Enigma code. His contribution to the allied war effort was priceless. The claim that his efforts shortened the Second World War by two years and saved millions of lives is quite reasonable. Unfortunately, the British authorities' rewarded Turing by treating him as a security risk because of his homosexuality. The widely held story of his death is that Turing committed suicide by eating a poisoned apple. Many of his friends and colleagues disagreed as he seemed happy and was excited by his current work. An alternative theory is that he accidentally consumed some cyanide that he was working with.

Only later was it commonly known that Turing knew the most top-secret secrets. In the lead up to his death, the security services considered Turing a risk with extensive knowledge of the government's most treasured secrets. Moreover, he was homosexual and could potentially be blackmailed. Guy Burgess and Donald Maclean, two homosexual spies who were also students at Cambridge, had recently defected to the Soviet Union. Still, Turing was an even greater threat. Alan Turing knew the government's most critical secrets and behaved eccentrically. As a result, the intelligence services tracked and hounded him. The codebreaking work at Bletchley Park was Ultra: far more hush-hush than nuclear weapons. So covert that even its existence was classified.

Since people did not know Turing's past, his peculiar death did not arouse suspicion. Dr Bird, the Macclesfield coroner, said it was a suicide while the balance of his mind was disturbed. [21] The coroner's comments in the hasty inquest were intriguing. Turing's body contained a huge dose of cyanide unlikely to have been consumed accidentally. Cyanide is notoriously toxic. A mere pinch (50-60mg) would be fatal. His "stomach contained four ounces of fluid that smelled very strongly of bitter almonds, as does a solution of cyanide". The conclusion? "Asphyxia due to cyanide poisoning. Death appeared to be due to violence". Accident, suicide, or assassination? It is unlikely that we will ever know what really happened.

Alan Turing could have an intense effect on people; his colleagues either liked him or hated him. He could be difficult and did not suffer fools gladly. Some computer engineers at Manchester University disliked him for years afterwards. In a way, one can see their point. Imagine being at the forefront of engineering and building one of the first digital computers, only to be overlooked and overshadowed. Turing was treated like a big shot, and no one would say why. Nobody could tell that Turing had done classified work in a hush-hush place and helped build a computer that was also above top secret. Then Turing brought the computer department into disrepute with his conviction for sexual offences. Even as late as the 1980s, some senior staff at Manchester University would play down his presence and contribution.

---

[21] The coroner's signature was difficult to read but appeared to be Bird.

Helping win World War Two was not Alan Turing's most outstanding achievement. Turing's single most significant contribution was the digital computer.[22] His description of the computer was a side issue. It was his response to a famous challenge to mathematicians about what could and could not be computed. Alonzo Church, a leading American mathematician, provided a more orthodox solution developing a new logic in the process. Turing's approach was more creative. He needed to show which numbers were computable – so he invented the computer!

Typically, Turing ignored what was known and worked things out for himself. He was unaware of Church's work and went back to basics. The computer Turing invented needed to calculate as well as any other device and be equal to the best computer possible.[23] But, of course, it wasn't a real computer but a highly simplified fantasy machine. It was totally impractical and just a figment of his imagination. Still, the idea has stimulated computer science ever since.

One of the issues was that back in 1936, when he published the paper,[24] the word computer usually referred to a young woman operating a mechanical adding machine. Employers preferred women because they were generally more careful than men, more accurate, and less costly to employ. At that time, few would have associated the word computer with a machine. Turing, however, was already interested in the possibility of building a brain. His idea was for a device that could think sufficiently well to tackle routine problems. Decades on, we live in a world of Turing machines. A small portable telephone can access the bulk of human knowledge, respond to a spoken question, and tell you how to navigate a map. Alan Turing showed how such things were possible, working only with paper and pencil.

The full implications of Turing's machine are often not realised. Turing's universal machine can simulate the most powerful supercomputer. You simply load the instructions needed to model

---

[22] Petzold C. (2008) The Annotated Turing, Wiley.
[23] Turing's machine was the equivalent of any physically realisable computer.
[24] Turing A.M. (1936) On computable numbers, with an application to the entscheidungsproblem, Proc. London Math. Soc., 42 (1), 230–265, (updated 1937).

the supercomputer and the relevant data. Set the universal Turing machine going, and it will produce the same output. The supercomputer is just faster.

Here we come to a critical finding. A computer is Turing complete if it is equivalent to Turing's universal machine. That is, it can work out anything capable of being computed. Of course, the device needs to have sufficient memory, the right program, and enough time to complete the task.

Importantly, all computers that reach a given level of complexity and become Turing complete are equivalent. This follows directly since a single universal machine can model any other computer.

All Turing machines are equivalent.

Turing's universal machine is not necessarily complicated; it just needs a minimum number of instructions and enough memory to hold all the data. Today nearly everything described as a computer is Turing complete. In 1956, the American computer engineer Claude Shannon had the idea of finding the minimal universal Turing machine with the smallest number of states and symbols. Surprisingly, a universal machine can be simple, perhaps four states, six symbols, and 22 instructions.[25] This device is hardly that complicated. Think in terms of describing the world's most powerful computer on the back of an envelope.

Turing machines can be simple.

While the minimalist nature of Turing complete sinks in, we can consider the big rainbow coloured elephant in the room.

## Machine Intelligence

Alan Turing's interest in the brain inspired his work on computing. Following the war, cybernetics guided his work, and he studied information in biology. He was a member of the Ratio Club of scientists, engineers, and mathematicians who investigated intelligent machines and animal behaviour. His ideas greatly influenced future work on artificial intelligence, including his

---

[25] Rogozhin Y. (1996) Small universal Turing machines, Theor. Comp. Sci., 168(2), 215-240.

anticipation of neural network computers. However, while Turing was inspirational, he published little of this research.

Turing explained how to view machine intelligence. He suggested a test that compared a conversation with a computer and a human. If you could not tell the machine from the human, it was reasonable to accept the computer to be reasonably 'intelligent', whatever that means. Turing's test had the contestants communicating at a distance over a teletype, the technology of the time. He defined intelligence as generating a conversation or other smart behaviour equivalent to that of a human. If it walks like a duck and quacks like a duck: you call it a duck.

Turing based his test on routine science. Experiment is the gold standard of science. A scientist is concerned with what he can observe, measure, and test. In this limited sense, a machine's intelligence is equivalent to that of a human if there is no way of telling them apart. Indistinguishable might be a more accurate word than equivalent.

Turing's imitation test was just a scientific comparison. He was not interested in testing for consciousness, the human spirit, or human genius; he left philosophers to specify such things. In Turing's words, "It is not possible to produce a set of rules purporting to describe what a man should do in every conceivable set of circumstances". Instead, we are concerned with approximation. As Turing put it, "We like to believe that Man is in some subtle way superior to the rest of creation. It is best if he can be shown to be necessarily superior, for then there is no danger of him losing his commanding position".

Turing was not trying to create a brilliant machine, just a mediocre one. He once joked to staff in the cafeteria at AT&T's Bell Labs that he just wanted to develop a dumb mechanical brain. In his high-pitched voice, he shouted that he hoped to build a brain merely as powerful as the President of AT&T. A device that could respond "Buy" or "Sell" at the appropriate time. History has fulfilled Turing's wish.[26] Artificially intelligent computers now run modern stock

---

[26] It is not clear that such stock market innovation is beneficial as it can add volatility.

markets. Unfortunately, humans are not fast enough to react to the massive streams of financial data.

Nowadays, computers commonly simulate things that people used to consider the unique domain of people. For example, computers can now analyse images and sounds. Not long ago, talking to a computer was science fiction. Now it is a commonplace occurrence. These days, some practical robots can respond to the environment and perform valuable tasks. Let us return to Spot, the robot dog. Naturally, a person would not mistake Spot for an actual biological dog. Still, Spot walks on four legs, avoids obstacles while running and jumping, and might smell its surroundings. Like a real dog, Spot might be trained to sit when you tell him. Over time, robotics engineers may develop robots that approximate more closely to a genuine dog's behaviour.

Philosophers may argue that these robot creatures do not have consciousness or real intelligence. Instead, we consider machine intelligence to be a form of basic cognition that could help an organism survive and reproduce – increase Darwinian fitness. In these terms, robots can adapt to their surroundings and even perform some activities beyond biology's capabilities. For example, birds don't fly at twice the speed of sound.

## Equivalence

*Natural selection removes organisms that are not Turing complete.*

An animal evolves the brain it needs for survival. The human brain may have more raw processing power than others do. Still, it turns out that this ability may be mostly irrelevant in evolutionary terms. Let us accept that the human brain is the supercomputer in biology. It is fast and has a massive memory. However, as described earlier, it is not known to be qualitatively superior to other brains. We can leave open the idea that at some point science will find a uniquely human ability, some aspect of creativity or genius perhaps.

In evolutionary terms, big brains have an evolutionary penalty. They use large amounts of energy. The human brain needs about 20% of all the oxygen required by the body, a most energy-demanding organ. Humans have taken the path of using their big brain's increased behavioural repertoire to offset the disadvantages of supporting the organ's energy needs. Other animals have also optimised their brain size according to their survival needs.

Now we may put this into the context Alan Turing provided. Most if not all animal brains are probably Turing complete. This statement seems an astonishing claim, but it does not mean a rabbit could play a game of chess as well as a human. We need to avoid such human-centric values. Chess is a human game constructed according to our abilities. Evolution programmed the rabbit's nervous system to dig holes in the right place, eat plants without getting sick, procreate, and avoid being eaten. The rabbit's brain matches the challenges of its environment.

An engineering analogy would be expecting a computer in a mobile phone to fly an aircraft. In principle, such control is possible, but we might want new software and a faster processor as part of a safe solution. Fortunately, Turing's imitation game suggests a fruitful approach.

To understand an organism, simulate its behaviour with a robot.

To obtain an idea of a rabbit's abilities, build a robotic rabbit with similar behaviour. From the rabbit point of view, a device is intelligent if it can behave like a rabbit. Still, making a robot rabbit is quite an engineering challenge. An engineer might find constructing the robots automatic controls demanding even with the most powerful computers. It is as least as challenging as building an electronic brain to imitate a person over a teletype. An engineer making a robot with legs for running, feet for digging, cameras for vision, microphones for sound, and chemical sampling for smell is just the start. That is the easy part.

The tricky part is reproducing the rabbit's ability to tie in and filter all these data inputs. We need image processing and analysis to recognise another rabbit and separate it from a fox. Similarly, hearing and real-time sound analysis are required. The robot needs to take fast, evasive action to avoid the fox. Can it reach the entrance to its hole in time? Can our robot rabbit accelerate quicker than the fox? How far away is the fox? Is our rabbit's top speed faster than that of the fox? Can it run for longer at speed? It needs a crude form of trigonometry to estimate the relative distances to the rabbit hole for the fox and itself. The terrain matters. Is the rabbit's path to its burrow clear, and is it smooth enough to support high speeds? Does the fox have a similarly clear track? There are thousands of equally challenging survival behaviours for the robot to simulate.

## Small But Sharp

Psychologists often consider chimp cognition, as they seem similar to humans. Going a little smaller, we might consider an insect. A butterfly has a parallel set of survival challenges. In some respects, it has more. The butterfly needs to fly, avoid predation, and find a mate of the same species but different sex. Finding a suitable mate could be difficult as it can take an experienced naturalist to separate some butterfly species. Furthermore, it has a different set of trials while growing as a caterpillar. Notice here we are allowing for only recognisable behaviour. The physiological changes from egg to caterpillar, caterpillar to pupa, and pupa to butterfly involve massive information processing. A new version of the operating system and software, if you will. We are moving far away from brains here, but the issues remain. Life at all resolutions involves computing.

Even smaller still, we have the microorganisms. An amoeba searches for prey like a science fiction blob. The amoeba sends out long appendages and pours itself in the required direction. What is more, these discriminating creatures have food preferences. They do not eat their own species but will consume other amoebae, indicating a form of self-recognition. Similarly, amoebae will not eat dead organisms. They prefer algae to diatoms but hunt ciliates in preference to algae.

Amoebae seem to be able to recognise their prey at some distance. One of their victims is the smaller but fast-moving paramecium. The amoeba starts its pursuit, targeting and stealthily approaching the quarry. This can be a tricky process as the paramecium can react far quicker than the amoeba. However, in grabbing its fast prey, the amoeba is working with some skill. A hunt may take 20 minutes or longer, during which the amoeba ignores other stimuli. The amoeba moves towards its target, slowly spreading out to remove escape pathways and using its body to trap its victim. Approaching it confirms the target is food, surrounds it, and wraps it in cell membrane. The amoeba closes up, squeezes, and consumes it in a process called phagocytosis.

Hunting is only one part of the amoebas living cycle of activity, feeding, and rest. Like larger animals, amoebae often take a rest period after eating. In this respect, this single-cell acts like some large animals or humans taking a siesta after lunch. The amoeba's marvellous daily life has been known for over 100 years since Oris Dellinger and David Gibbs recorded a number of days of the microbe's activity.[27]

In Clark University labs in 1905, they spent several days and nights continuously following amoebae with a microscope. They also worked for weeks monitoring a single specimen. As they put it, the amoeba "must take its place in the true animal series with the rudiments at least of true animal behaviour".

Several white blood cells have similar amoeboid behaviour. They learn and adapt to changing conditions. In our bodies, the macrophage is a type of white blood cell involved in the immune response. Macrophages patrol our tissues and organs and have many amoeba-like properties. They travel around searching for microbes, other foreign bodies, and cell debris. These white cells need mechanisms to recognise healthy cells and separate them from invaders. A macrophage finding an invader surrounds and gobbles it up in amoeba-like phagocytosis.

When Dellinger and Gibbs changed the amoeba's food source, it adapted. However, some amoebae were slow and took several days to adjust. This delay was more apparent when they had to hunt new prey more actively. Amoebae were able to target and pursue a single paramecium. However, some were unable to make the transition to more complex hunting behaviour. A few amoebae seemed confused when surrounded by a crowd of paramecia. They ignored being bumped about by their prey, seemingly unable to process all the data. Others simply took their usual blob-like form and moved off.

By contrast, the amoeba's prey struggled to get away from the predator and avoid being eaten. In its turn, the paramecium was also hunting for even smaller organisms such as bacteria, algae or yeast that it would recognise and eat. Paramecium moves using cilia, tiny

---

[27] Gibbs D. Dellinger O. (1908). The daily life of amœba proteus, Am. J. of Psychol., 19(2), 232-241.

hairs that cover its body in closely spaced rows. The cilia whip about in close coordination like the wind passing over a field of corn. If a paramecium bumps into something, it changes direction rather like a robot programmed to avoid obstacles. The paramecium reverses, turns through an angle and tries to move forward again. It repeats the operation to get around the obstruction. [28] Paramecia also show an ability for simple learning, such as separating light and dark.[29,30] Notably, even the tiny bacterium at the end of this microbial food chain displays surprising behaviour.

Bacteria are a diverse lot and have surprising behaviours. Some bacteria are motile and move about using flagella, long whip-like cilium. These and other motile bacteria sense their surroundings. Some bacteria use touch to recognise larger cells they can infect.[31] Bacteria move away from toxins and towards valuable substances such as food, a process called chemotaxis. The method starts with proteins in the bacterial membrane. These receptor proteins recognise different chemicals. If the receptor binds to a chemical, it transmits a message or signal to the cell and flagella. The flagella respond by moving the bacterium towards or away from the chemical.

## What Does It Take To Be Smart?

Software engineer Skeptic Sam suggests that animals are not that smart. Take bird navigation. Skeptic Sam says he could make a suitable model aircraft soar like a gull finding thermals off a cliff. Sam understands that it is a demanding project. Landing and take-off in high winds and varied environments might be tricky. The software would need to be adaptive and employ machine learning. But, even if Sam has an inflated opinion of his skills, we should take his claims seriously.

---

[28] Ogura A. Takahashi K. (1976) Artificial deciliation causes loss of calcium-dependent responses in Paramecium, Nature, 264, 170–172.
[29] Ginsburg S. Jablonka E. (2009) Epigenetic learning in non-neural organisms, J. Biosci., 34(4), 633-46.
[30] Abolfazl A. *et al* (2017) Possible molecular mechanisms for paramecium learning, J. Advanced Medical Sciences and Applied Technologies, 3 (1), 39-46.
[31] Hug I. *et al* (2017) Second messenger–mediated tactile response by a bacterial rotary motor, Science, 358(6362), 531-534.

Sam had read how gulls navigate around the Atlantic Ocean without GPS or even a map. In principle, Sam thought he could even get a suitable model aircraft to navigate an ocean. He could get it to return close to the starting point using the sun, the earth's magnetic field, and sniffing chemicals released from the sea. There is no magic. Bird navigation is just a rather challenging project.

I agree with Sam that it is a demanding computing project. But could Sam do it if the programming language wasn't Turing complete? In other words, the question is could the simulation work successfully with missing logic? There are a reasons computers and mainstream programming languages are Turing complete: they need to be practical and versatile enough to be useful. It is unlikely that Turing incomplete software could help an engineer simulate gull navigation, an immune system, or a brain.

We will find biocomputing suggests that even microorganisms are capable of this level of logic. As described later, even single cells can perform basic logical operations. Scientists do not know which organisms are Turing complete – they haven't been looking. Still, we can state as a reasonable hypothesis:

All living organisms are Turing complete.

Even simple cell division demands a fantastic amount of control. This capacity is not apparent because people think of computing and intelligence in terms of human requirements. Similarly, the adaptations organisms need for evolutionary success are not obvious. A fish does not need submarine technology. A butterfly does not require a degree in aeronautical engineering. Likewise, our gull does not need a sat nav. Still, they can swim, fly, and navigate journeys of thousands of miles. Furthermore, they achieve these things with an efficiency unequalled by human equipment.

## Different Ways of Living

If humans underestimate animal behaviour, they are even less familiar with microorganisms and their environmental demands. Microorganisms also engage in the struggle for survival. However, the challenges microorganisms' face differ in detail from that of large animals. They live in what we might describe as a thick viscous gel and are battered about by thermal motions. Microorganisms have different, more primitive senses than animals. Still, they have survived and thrived for millions of years in a frantic world of chemistry, touch, and light. The microbial world is quite alien to our senses.

Bacteria can respond using swarm intelligence, which is also unfamiliar to humans who have invested their behavioural capacity in a single large brain. For similar reasons, engineers built the early computers around a single processor. They could make a faster computer by increasing the processor speed or adding quicker memory. As a result, computers developed rapidly according to what engineers called Moore's law. The popular version of Moore's law was that processor speeds and processing power would double every two years. The idea was empirical and reflected improvements in manufacturing. However, there are limits to speed in a computer chip, such as quantum physics and the increasingly minute size of transistors.

One approach to computer speed is to replace a single computer with multiple processors working in parallel. For some problems, it is easy to split a calculation into separate streams. Take calculating the total area of forests in the world. It would be much faster if a different individual did the estimation for each country. Then again, you might break the country down into states or blocks and assign someone to each local area, gaining even more speed. Parallel processing works well for problems where there is no crosstalk between the different parts. However, it is not so good if the local calculation depends on other parts of the problem.

## Parallel Computing and Swarms

Small size and limited logic does not limit bacterial intelligence. To what extent a single bacterium comes close to being Turing complete is unknown. However, this does not mean these microbes lack intelligence.

Bacteria process data as a swarm.

If we take parallel processing to its limit, we have numerous but very simple computing elements. John Conway developed a way of looking at this extreme parallel computing using a computer game, the game of life. The world of the game is a grid of square cells on a computer screen. A cell is alive or dead depending on its colour, black or white.

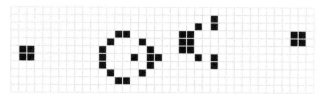

Gosper glider gun in the game of life[32]

Each cell is independent but can react to its immediate eight neighbours. The cells respond simply with each step of the game.

1.  A live cell with two or three live neighbours survives; otherwise, it dies.
2.  A dead cell becomes alive if it has three live neighbours.

It is difficult at face value to see how you could program Conway's game to solve a real problem, but it can be done with a lot of effort. Surprisingly, this game is Turing complete as it can simulate a computer. Paul Rendell showed that it is possible to construct a Turing machine within the game and watch it computing. The difficulty of thinking about how this might be achieved reflects the biologist's understanding of how bacteria or other microorganisms can think.

Swarms of dumb objects can be Turing complete.

Cells in Conway's game of life have a couple of simple rules. By contrast, the behaviour of individual microorganisms is far more impressive, which indicates a swarm could also be Turing complete. Moreover, it turns out that Conway's game is a particular example of a form of cellular automata described by Stanislaw Ulam and John von Neumann. Such cellular automata are a simple model of parallel computing.

John von Neumann suggested scientists could use cellular automata to study self-replication – machines that build themselves. He was aiming to have a better understanding of living organisms.

---

[32] Bill Gosper's 1970 glider gun was the first known finite pattern with unbounded growth.

Much later, Andrew Wade made a self-reproducing pattern in the game of life.[33] In other words, a logical design can reproduce itself somewhat like a living creature.[34] Once again, the difficulty in creating a self-replicating pattern illustrates the logic involved when bacteria and other cells replicate.

So swarms of simple organisms can process information, and we might expect them to be smart. Let's take a practical example. Doctors famously extracted an antibiotic drug from the mould Penicillium notatum. Penicillin stops some bacteria from building their cell walls, preventing them from dividing and growing.

Penicillin was one of the first antibiotics introduced into medicine and started a revolution in fighting infectious diseases. Leading doctors claimed that antibiotics meant that they had beaten bacterial infections; bacterial disease was a thing of the past. Human brilliance and medical technology had won this war. Scientists quickly introduced additional antibiotics, and medicine consolidated its dominance. The story was that science could keep a steady introduction of these drugs, meaning it would be practically impossible for bacteria to evolve and become resistant.

Now penicillin was a substance that bacteria knew well. For millions of years, fungi had attacked them with the drug. The same was true of many other antibiotics. Bacteria in soil, such as Streptomyces griseus, secreted streptomycin. Similarly, chemists developed tetracycline from a bacterial secretion, e.g. Streptomyces aureofaciens. Medicine had not created the antibiotics merely discovered them being used by organisms they considered dumb.

Typical disease-causing bacteria did not carry the biochemistry critical to producing a response to these antibiotics. They thrive on efficiency. Bacteria keep things simple and retain only those genes needed for survival. If bacteria have not fought off penicillin for generations, most will ditch the genes required to deal with it. It takes energy to keep maintaining the genes and making copies of them every time they divide. Fast growth and division are central to bacterial survival strategy, fighting antibiotics not so much.

---

[33] Aron J. (2010) First replicating creature spawned in life simulator, New Scientist, 16 June.
[34] Perhaps we need to point out to some that the replicating systems do not need DNA.

Bacteria would occasionally run into a penicillin producing mould. The antibiotic would generally be isolated and of little significance to the widespread bacteria. This changed when medicine and agriculture started using antibiotics with abandon. Sadly, however, medicine had not beaten the bacteria. All they achieved was increased antibiotic pressure. The bacteria responded accordingly.

Bacteria had several methods of dealing with penicillin. A quick response was to change their current behaviour.[35] Firstly, bacteria would typically multiply, as this is their evolutionary imperative. These rapidly growing bacteria are immediately affected by penicillin. However, despite being genetically identical and in the same environment, a proportion of bacteria would be dividing slowly or even dormant. The antibiotic would have a limited effect on these slow-growing cells as they were not producing new cell walls. Thus, some cells electing for slow growth meant the colony could survive a period of antibiotic attack. Bacteria varying their behaviour in this way is a standard survival approach.[36]

We noted that disease-causing bacteria would ditch genes that were currently of no use. They do not need to carry them, as a bacterium can pick up a parcel of genes at any time. Bacteria share genetic information. They release plasmids or circles of DNA that contain the instructions for building proteins. Swapping plasmids gives bacteria a massive memory capacity. The plasmid instructions are just data, and the process is logically equivalent to sharing computer files. In this case, the genetic instructions were for beating antibiotics.

Notably, a single plasmid might confer resistance to not just one drug but a range of antibiotics. A bacterium could become multidrug-resistant in an instant and rapidly proliferate to form a vast population. The doctors did not expect this response. Doctors believed bacterial comeback was limited to conventional evolution mechanisms. They thought that the bacteria would respond slowly

---

[35] Balaban N.Q. *et al* (2004) Bacterial persistence as a phenotypic switch, Science, 305(5690), 1622-1625.
[36] Dhar N. McKinney J.D. (2007) Microbial phenotypic heterogeneity and antibiotic tolerance, Curr. Opin. Microbiol., 10(1), 30-38.

based on mutation and natural selection. Had that been the case, it might have taken millennia for bacteria to mount such an effective response.

The bacterial reply was impressive. Bacteria are promiscuous. Not only do bacteria share genes, but they also share genes between species. In principle, there is no difference between plasmids from different bacteria and no species barrier, rather like an ant having sex with a wombat and giving birth to a host of wombants. For the microorganisms, this is a standard way of dealing with survival problems across their whole ecology.

If one organism worked out a solution, it could protect all associated bacteria. This information transfer is, of course, not limited to just antibiotics and other threats. For example, it might transfer genes for living on a different foodstuff. The bacteria had a worldwide information-sharing web. Medicine wasn't fighting a particular disease-causing bug with antibiotics. It was trying to take on the microorganisms as a whole.

The mistake that medicine made was to underestimate the abilities of bacteria. They considered bacteria dumb, but the microbial response was sophisticated. Game set and match to the bugs. Bacterial computing had taken an unexpected form, like patterns moving in the game of life. We can state another hypothesis in this context as:

Any organism can be as intelligent as any other.

This hypothesis applies only if the organism is Turing complete, but this is a low bar. We might equally ask what organism is not Turing complete. If evolution pushed an organism in this direction, it would become Turing complete. The question is how evolution has programmed the system rather than the capacity of a particular wibbly-wobbly biocomputer.

## The Bacterial Brain

In biological terms, high-speed processing is central to the human brain. It helps people identify potential predators quickly, giving time for a life-saving response. Brains are a fast computing solution for individual survival. At the other end of the scale, bacteria have limited individuality.

Microorganisms are generally self-similar, ubiquitous and rapidly dividing to produce identical copies of themselves. The loss of a single individual in a billion clones is hardly critical. It is not clear that bacteria need a brain's fast response to protect an individual. Besides, it is not evident what a rapid response would mean in this context. The individual might only exist for a few minutes before it becomes two. Alternatively, it might form a spore.

A bacterial spore can shut off its metabolism to undetectable levels. In this dormant form, it can endure extreme challenges to survival. For example, it might survive boiling in bleach, intense pressure, and high-energy radiation. Importantly, dormant bacteria can survive for millennia and revive.[37] Thus, our understanding of time as large organisms may have little relevance to bacteria.

Fast and frugal living bacteria have no use for a brain. Instead, they process information on their own survival timescale. Bacteria have been around for hundreds of millions of years, while the dinosaurs and other species came and went. Humans hardly affect them at all. Bacteria are likely to continue into the distant future long after the species Homo sapiens has gone extinct.

---

[37] Cano R.J. Borucki M.K. (1995) Revival and identification of bacterial spores in 25- to 40-million-year-old Dominican amber, Science, 268 (5213), 1060–1064.

"We are not interested in the fact that the brain has the consistency of cold porridge".

Alan Turing

# Biocomputing

"All I ask is that we compare human consciousness with spirochete ecology".

Lynn Margulis

In an attempt to use a computer to show the power of natural selection Richard Dawkins unwittingly demonstrated its weakness. The physicist Fred Hoyle and others had pointed out the astronomical implausibility of chance assembling a large protein. This concern is known as the watchmaker's problem; a watch does not simply build itself. Find a watch in the woods, and you know someone made it. It seems too complicated and functional to arise by chance alone. Notably, the simplest cell is far more complex than a timepiece. Hoyle stated that the origin of life on earth is comparable to "the chance that a tornado sweeping through a junkyard might assemble a Boeing 747". Hoyle's is an excellent illustration but not really true – life is far less likely.

Fred Hoyle was challenging the story of the monkey and the typewriter. Given enough time, the monkey would type out the complete works of Shakespeare by chance alone. This is true, but a mathematician's infinite time is not a practical explanation. So instead, the monkey story paraphrases Darwin's gradualism, where small changes generate new species over a geologically long period.

Dawkins started his investigation by making the problem more manageable. Instead of Shakespeare's complete works, Dawkins used the phrase "Methinks it is like a weasel" from Hamlet. Dawkins exchanged for this much easier problem because the string of letters is so short, only 28 characters. Moreover, he then further simplified by restricting the keyboard to only 26 capitals and the space bar.[38] It is a vastly more manageable problem, but a brute force attack is still extremely unlikely to succeed.

---

[38] There are $27^{28}$ i.e. about $10^{40}$ possibilities.

Dawkins described how he had programmed his microcomputer to search randomly for the string. The computer solved the problem over lunch. His was a 1980s computer; your mobile phone could probably solve the problem in seconds using the same method (if it were a slow machine). So there you are, natural selection wins – or does it?

It just doesn't seem right. Dawkins seems to be evading the laws of mathematics. The banks use long strings of digits to protect their funds online with evident success. Similarly, ordinary people use passwords to safeguard themselves. The idea is the same; it takes a long time to guess the string of characters. Our modern world depends on such security. So how had Dawkins achieved his remarkable result, and do we need to develop new online security urgently?

Surprisingly, it was entirely expected that Dawkins would achieve his result in a short time. It turns out that Dawkins made the problem much easier by introducing a target and a fitness function. He was feeding the result he wanted into the program as a guide. The program started with a random string and mutated (changed at random) the characters. It compared the new string with the target and kept the characters that were closer to the result. The computer was processing the data and comparing the latest output with the answer he wanted. Dawkins described the program as cumulative selection. He claimed this was similar to natural selection.

Dawkins had introduced a fitness function that was the opposite of his ideas of how natural selection works. In other words, at each step, he was asking how close we are to the result we want. It seemed easy because Dawkins was using supervised learning.[39] Supervised learning is when the program has a target. Rather amusingly, you might equally say he introduced an aim or purpose. Think about it, the program knew the required result in advance, which massively reduces the search space. It is the equivalent of your bank helping hackers by allowing repeated tries to type the password and telling them whenever they get one of the characters right!

Natural selection is a consequence of fitness.

---

[39] Dangeti P. (2017) Statistics for Machine Learning, Packt Publishing.

In another sense, Dawkins had indirectly shown something important. Fitness is the critical thing for natural selection, even over a geological time scale. A suitable fitness function speeds up evolution. With an appropriate target guiding the fitness, Hoyle's objection does not apply. The evolutionary target is an organism's need to eat, survive, and reproduce.

Evolution depends on organisms aiming to survive and reproduce.

By my estimate, without the target, Dawkins would still be searching for a solution, even if his computer were a million times faster. That might still be the case had he started at the big bang at the beginning of the universe. That's how internet security works.

## Hidden Logic

Two French scientists Francois Jacob and Jacques Monod demonstrated that bacteria had evolved simple logic to help them eat efficiently. First, they studied how bacteria responded to sugars. Most organisms use glucose to store and transport chemical energy. While they prefer glucose, bacteria consume other sugars, including lactose the sugar in milk. Next, Jacob and Monod showed how E. coli bacteria use logic to switch genes ON or OFF according to which sugar was available.

One of the scientists, Jacques Monod, had a philosophical bent and tried to remove mind and purpose from biology.[40] He thought evolution and life were a result of pure chance. Monod thought E. coli's choice of sugar was merely apparent, and there was no intentionality. Indeed, there was no real choice, as the bacterium must act in this way. In this sense, the bacterium's intelligent behaviour was just an emergent result of a reductionist process. The process was mechanical, and the gene switching just happened.

Glucose is the most widely available sugar and is easy to metabolise. However, lactose is more challenging than glucose; it consists of two simple sugars bonded together. So firstly, a new protein is required to pump lactose into the cell. Then the bacterium needs an enzyme called lactase to split lactose and release its two sugars, glucose and galactose. But, of course, the bacterium does not

---

[40] Monod J. (1972) Chance and Necessity, Harper Collins.

want to waste energy making these proteins if it doesn't have lactose. So it keeps their genes switched off until needed.

From our point of view, the bacteria implement a set of simple instructions that we can write in computer pseudocode

If glucose

    Switch lactose genes OFF

Else

    If lactose

        Switch lactose genes ON

    Else

        Switch lactose genes OFF

    End if

End if

The biochemistry is straightforward. When lactose is present, the cell forms allolactose. Allolactose switches the lactose genes ON. Otherwise, the bacterium keeps the lactose genes switched OFF. Similarly, when glucose is present, it generates another molecule called cAMP that switches the lactose genes OFF. The outcome is the E. coli bacterium eats its preferred glucose but efficiently switches to lactose when necessary.

As Monod stated, it is a simple mechanical process. But so is every logical step in the most advanced machine intelligence or the internet. A modern AI system is just an arrangement of logical operations. Jacob and Monod's control mechanism may be simple but produced apparently purposeful and smart behaviour.

It is not difficult to develop a narrative whereby evolution could lead to such logic "circuits". We are familiar with the ideas of hardware and software. The wetware of biocomputing is a little different. With wetware, there is no clear distinction between software programs and hardware. No programmer is necessary. Similar self-learning machine intelligence systems have been around for decades.[41] If it makes it easier, imagine natural selection acting to produce simple logic and survival behaviour.

Much of wetware occurs at the level of protein molecules. An enzyme is a protein that speeds up, or catalyses, a reaction. Many substances can block an enzyme's action. So, for example, penicillin binds to an enzyme bacteria use to build their cell walls. When attached in this way, the enzyme no longer functions effectively. We can describe this in logical terms as

Enzyme AND NOT penicillin … THEN bacterial cell walls

Enzyme AND penicillin … THEN NOT bacterial cell walls

This logic is a less usual approach to enzyme biochemistry. Still, it makes the point that we can think of penicillin as an ON-OFF switch for bacterial cell wall manufacture. There are many similar cases where the presence of a cofactor activates an enzyme. Consider Enzyme A working with cofactor B

IF Enzyme-A AND B THEN C.

An enzyme inhibitor D works in the opposite way

IF Enzyme-A AND D THEN NOT C

Medicines often act with a similar logic. Drugs work by attaching to receptors on the surface of cells. Receptors evolved to receive chemical signals that drugs mimic. The drug is a message that tells the cell to respond by altering its internal biochemistry and behaviour.

Hormones work in a like manner and are also signalling molecules. Indeed, signalling and receptors have a long evolutionary history; they are on the amoeba's surface, helping control its behaviour. Similarly, bacteria use receptors to gain information about their environment. Moreover, microorganisms can retain some of these input signals to provide a memory. Denis Bray, a computational biologist at Cambridge, described bacterial estimation of a changing chemical signal as performing calculus.[42]

We should beware of assuming that the digital logic in computers occurs in cells in the same way. In some cases, the information is clear: DNA employs a form of digital encoding. However, cells are

---

[41] Deisenroth M.P. (2020) Mathematics for Machine Learning, Cambridge Univ. Press.
[42] Bray D. (2009) Wetware, Yale Univ. Press.

more likely to be described by analog computing, responding smoothly to signals. Cells will use whatever methods are available – evolution rewards solutions that work efficiently. Turing's logic still applies, but the implementation is wibbly-wobbly wetware rather than silicon.

Cells are wetware.

These simplified examples show how biocomputing can be achieved. Indeed, we can rephrase much of modern biochemistry in these terms. Cells are engaged in real-time logic, signal, and data processing. In this way, the cell is a mass of cybernetic controls that continuously process information.

## Basic Wetware

Biocomputing asks how a watery microscopic blob can search, hunt, avoid predators, and reproduce. Bacteria can move in straight lines or flip directions. Different bacteria demonstrate individuality in their movements. This variation is not genetic as the bacteria contain the same DNA and appear identical in structure. Some tumble more often or move further in straight lines. Nevertheless, the bacteria can alter their flipping rate to change direction and move away from a harmful chemical.

In 1902, an American biologist Herbert Spencer Jennings noted the difference in behaviour between motile microorganisms, like paramecium, which typically rushes about, and those with a fixed position.[43] Jennings published a book a few years later on the activities of microorganisms.[44] His experiments illustrate the extraordinary behaviour of these tiny creatures.

Jennings worked with the trumpet-shaped Stentor roeseli to see how it would respond to irritation. Stentor is a single-celled horn-shaped creature with a wide mouth that attaches to plants by its narrow end. Cilia around the mouth trap bacteria and other small microorganisms. Jennings gave Stentor indigestible particles of dye

---

[43] Jennings H.S. (1902) Studies on reactions to stimuli in unicellular organisms ix, on the behavior of fixed infusoria (stentor and vorticella), with special reference to the modifiability of protozoan reactions, Am. J. Physiology, 8(1), 23-60.
[44] Jennings H.S. (1906) Behavior of the Lower Organisms, Columbia Univ. Press.

with a micropipette. Stentor twisted away and spat out the particles by reversing its cilia or pulling back from the stimulus.

As Jennings continued, Stentor would detach itself and swim away to avoid the irritating biologist. Stentor modified its behaviour depending on the level of annoyance. It adapted, changing its mind and finding another way of responding. Previously biologists considered only much larger animals could have such adaptive behaviour. Over the years, however, some biologists tried to replicate Jennings work without success, and they discounted his results.

In 2019, Jeremy Gunawardena, a systems biologist at Harvard, examined Stentor closely and confirmed its sophisticated behaviour.[45] He repeated Jenning's experiment and found that he had been right. In Gunawardena's words, Stentor "have to be 'clever' at figuring out what to avoid, where to eat and all the other things that organisms have to do to live".

When considering replication failures, one thing to keep in mind is that some experimenters are far more skilful than the average. For example, it turned out that an earlier study claiming to repeat Jennings work in 1967 had difficulty finding the same species of Stentor, so they studied Stentor coeruleus instead.[46] But, unfortunately, they had chosen a more mobile species that just swam away from irritants.

Gunawardena's study produced more exciting findings. For example, Stentor decided to swim away based on the equivalent of a coin toss. The probability is almost 50-50, but the mechanism is unknown. Gunawardena explains that "cells exist in a very complex ecosystem, and they are, in a way, talking and negotiating with each other, responding to signals and making decisions".

At this point, we can introduce another conjecture:

The size of an organism does not dictate its need for cognition.

Dinosaur's and microorganisms alike need to move, find suitable habitat, search for food, avoid predators, distinguish their own

---

[45] Dexter J.P *et al* (2019) A complex hierarchy of avoidance behaviours in a single-cell eukaryote, Current Biology, 29(24), 4323-4329.
[46] https://phys.org/news/2019-12-single-celled-mind.html, accessed Jan 2020.

species, and find a suitable mate. Just because a creature is small does not mean life is easy.

## Neural Networks

Searching for logic in cells and organisms is likely to be only partly successful. A similar problem exists with artificial neural networks. While the details vary with the simulation, an artificial neural network is a model of the brain. Computer engineers connect simple representations of neurons to form a network. The approach seems more advanced than it actually is, as you can build a neural network with limited programming skills. People should not take the idea of brain simulation too far.

A leading electronics company had built a rudimentary neural network computer chip some time ago and asked for my opinion about its potential applications. To work within the limits of the silicon, the designer had built a simple binary network. A simulated nerve cell was little more than a bit, an ON/OFF switch triggered by randomised connections. The designer thought he had a chip that worked like the brain. When I asked if he really believed that, he treated my question with incomprehension. "Yes, of course. How else would the brain work?"

My reply was that even single nerve cells are immensely complicated, and biology is not easily understood. It was likely that the entire neural network chip was not capable of replicating a single neuron. There were some practical applications for the chip, but they were limited. Understandably, the contract went to an international software company that waxed lyrical about the wonderful new development and their ability to find applications. I never heard that the chip found any practical use.

The positives of artificial neural networks are that they are easy to build and easy to train. They learn from examples and can produce some sophisticated decision making. Applications are diverse and include face recognition, reading car license plates, or estimating the risk of giving someone a loan. Neural networks are a basic but practical approach to machine learning. A limitation is that it is difficult to know what they are doing or why they are doing it. There are no simple logic statements for programmers to follow. The processing is distributed in parallel and contains a random element. Imagine a giant ball of dynamically changing spaghetti logic.

The difficulty of following the processing in an artificial neural network suggests we look for similar atypical logic in biocomputing. Humans chose standard digital computer logic to be relatively easy to work with, understand, and follow. Silicon and our use of language and mathematics are also constraints. Living cells are not so limited and use any methods in parallel to solve problems.

In the same way, trying to follow what a human brain is doing is outside the realm of current science. For example, the brain has about the same number of nerve cells as stars in the Milky Way.[47] However, the number of synaptic connections is hundreds of times greater, generating an almost inconceivably massive number of logical pathways. Similarly, there are many glial cells in the brain making up a substantial proportion of the tissue. Still, neuroscientists usually ignore the glia and their impressive ability to process information.[48]

In approaching biological cognition, we ask whether Kanzi the bonobo understands the language he has been trained to use in the same way humans do. This question seems superficially reasonable since bonobos and chimps are our closest living relatives. However, bonobos have a different evolutionary imperative and might consider acrobatics in trees a more adequate intelligence test.[49]

---

[47] DeWeerdt S. (2019) How to map the brain, Nature.com, 24 July, accessed Jan 2021.
[48] Fields R.D. (2011) The Other Brain, Simon and Schuster.
[49] Consider the difficulty of building a robot bonobo to traverse treetops – possible but impressively computationally demanding.

"If you really want to study evolution, you've got go outside sometime, because you'll see symbiosis everywhere!"

Lynn Margulis

# Darwin's Theory

*"The strange thing about the theory of evolution is that everyone thinks he understands it. But we do not".*

Stuart Kauffman

Charles Darwin is the most celebrated biologist in history. His ideas on evolution are the core of our understanding of the science of life. Darwin took the idea of natural selection and used it to describe the development of life on this planet. Ordinary people became aware of natural selection following his bestselling book The Origin of Species, published in 1859. Darwin's fame and reputation rest mainly on this work, but he would have been historically significant even without evolution. Interestingly, some claim Darwin was one of the most outstanding scientists who ever lived. By contrast, others consider him just a plodder.

As biologist Adam Wilkins put it, "The case for Darwin as genius is straightforward". "His development of the concept of natural selection and his arguments for it as the motor of evolution were brilliant".[50] Still, reading my edition of Darwin's Origin, I came across a strange and usually ignored statement. "In 1831 Mr Patrick Matthew published his work on 'Naval Timber and Arboriculture' in which he gave precisely the same view on the origin of species as...Mr Wallace and myself". But it "remained unnoticed until now". So Darwin told us that some guy called Patrick Matthew published the complete theory of natural selection almost three decades earlier.

Following The Origin's initial success, Scottish farmer and landowner Patrick Matthew pointed out that the theory of evolution by natural selection was his idea. To his credit, Darwin quickly agreed. "I freely acknowledge that Mr Matthew has anticipated by many years the explanation which I have offered of the origin of species, under the name of natural selection".[51] Darwin accepted that Matthew's book had explained natural selection long before.

---

[50] Wilkins A.S. (2009) Charles Darwin: Genius or plodder? Genetics, 183(3), 773-777.

We should remember that Darwin had no choice but to accept that priority for natural selection should go to Patrick Matthew. After all, Darwin could hardly claim that Matthew's book did not exist. But many of Darwin's later followers were not as honest. They could make great efforts to hide and minimise Matthew's contribution. Unfortunately, some people appear to need Darwin as their hero genius and avoid properly giving credit where it is due.

Some have claimed that Patrick Matthew did not appreciate the importance of the discovery and did not announce it more widely. However, the counter-argument is that he might have considered Darwin's narrative an obvious development. In his words, "this law of nature came intuitively as a self-evident fact". It was "an axiom requiring only to be pointed out to be admitted by unprejudiced minds of sufficient grasp". In other words, Matthew explained natural selection, and the rest should have been immediately understood.

Historians and Darwin's biographers should be aware that Matthew was the originator of evolution by natural selection. However, the priority discussion is mainly limited to whether Alfred Wallace or Charles Darwin deserves the credit.[52] A recent extensive biography of Darwin does mention Patrick Matthew. He is a "curmudgeonly" "timber merchant" with socialist ideas who wanted votes for commoners.[53] Matthew was a "Malthusian evolutionist". It states, "Like Darwin's, Matthew's social and organic evolution were all of a piece". Which would seem to be a begrudging admission that Matthew deserves recognition for natural selection's discovery.

Ironically, the process of misappropriating credit is called the Matthew Effect after Patrick Matthew's biblical namesake. We can further add to the irony with the prolonged use of evolution to attack religion. The original Bible quote is, "Whoever has will be given more, and they will have an abundance. Whoever does not have, even what they have will be taken from them".[54] In science, the

---

[51] Darwin C. (1860) Letter, Gardeners' Chronicle and Agricultural Gazette, April.
[52] Ginnobili S. Blanco D. (2019) Wallace's and Darwin's natural selection theories, Synthese, 196, 991–1017.
[53] Desmond A. Moore J. (1991) Darwin, Michael Joseph.
[54] Matthew 13, 11-12, Bible, New International Version

Matthew Effect describes how credit is taken from the lowly experimenter and given to eminent scientists who are already famous.[55]

The popularity of Darwin's Origin contrasts with the meagre reception to Alfred Wallace's paper and Darwin's unpublished notes presented to the Linnean Society the previous year. Wallace had sent his evolution paper to Darwin, knowing he would be interested. Darwin later claimed that Wallace's views were similar to his own, but there were significant differences. For example, Darwin emphasised competition, with animals contending with each other and only the fittest surviving. Many follow this competitive approach. However, Alfred Wallace took a somewhat different and broader viewpoint; a fit animal adapts to its environment.

According to Wallace, natural selection was also a way of maintaining the stability of species. Indeed, this was a widespread view at the time.[56] As the fossil record shows, species can stay the same for millions of years despite genetic and random drift. Natural selection can act to maintain permanence. It keeps the species a steady match for its environment. When the environment changes, natural selection alters the organism to match the new situation. Surprising to some, the stability of species is as profound a problem as species change. For Wallace, natural selection was about control. The origin of species was just one aspect of the mechanism.

There is some doubt about when Darwin received Wallace's paper. He seems to have lost or destroyed the letter and envelope, which would have indicated the date. It also appears that Darwin may have given the wrong dates.[57] Nevertheless, Darwin's influential friends, geologist Sir Charles Lyell and botanist Sir Joseph Hooker took an unusual step. They presented Wallace's paper to the Linnean Society with an extract of an unpublished essay and a letter Darwin wrote to ensure he shared credit for the idea.[58] This was a questionable process with the explicit aim of Darwin sharing credit.[59]

---

[55] Merton R. (1968) Science, 159(3810), 56-63.
[56] Gould S.J. (2002) The Structure of Evolutionary Theory, Harvard Univ. Press.
[57] Uchii S. (2004) Darwin's principle of divergence, paper presented at the 5th Quadrennial International Fellows Conference (inRytro, Poland), May 26-30.
[58] Darwin C.R. Wallace A.R. (1858) On the tendency of species to form varieties; and on the perpetuation of varieties and species by natural means of selection, J. Proc. Linnean Soc. London, Zoology, 3(9), 45-62.

Still, they were aware Darwin had been privately floating ideas about selection and evolution for some time.

Notably, Lyell and Hooker presented the paper with Darwin's name first. Without consulting Wallace, they made Darwin a co-author, actually the lead author. Sadly, the authorship also emphasised the difference in status. "By Charles Darwin, Esq., F.R.S., F.L.S., & F.G.S., and Alfred Wallace, Esq". Moreover, Darwin's two extracts with earlier dates precede Wallace's paper in their presentation. An artful Darwin washed his hands of the dubious process. He wrote to Wallace, "I had absolutely nothing whatever to do in leading Lyell and Hooker to do what they thought a fair course of action".

The scientific community was at first unimpressed with natural selection and had a muted response. Besides, ideas about evolution were not new but part of scientific thought going back centuries. Wallace had already published the background ideas but without natural selection as the final piece of the jigsaw.[60,61]

The Zoologist reviewed the presentations in terms of current biology. Thomas Boyd suggested it lacked supporting data. The theory "starts upon the smallest possible basis of facts, the known variation in species, and then goes on, without any additional fact, to the possibility or probability of an indefinite extension of this variation".

In other words, Boyd considered it a weak and speculative hypothesis. He continued, "Is this wise! Is it in accordance with the spirit of modern Science?"[62] Boyd found the whole approach questionable.

Similarly, in the same journal, Arthur Hussey suggested that the theory is "founded upon the imaginary probable, rather than

[59] Eg: Brackman A. (1980) A Delicate Arrangement, Times Books.
[60] Wallace A.R. (1855) On the law which has regulated the introduction of new species, Annals and Magazine of Natural History, 16, 184-196
[61] Van Wyhe J. (2016) The impact of A. R. Wallace's Sarawak Law paper reassessed, Studies in History and Philosophy of Science Part C: Studies in History and Philosophy of Biological and Biomedical Sciences, 60, 56-66.
[62] Boyd T. (1859) Review, Zoologist, 17, 6357-6359.

obtained by induction from ascertained facts".[63] Again, Hussey thought it an imaginative indulgence.

Finally, Thomas Bell, President of the Linnean Society, added his comments. "The year…has not…been marked by any of those striking discoveries which at once revolutionise…the…science". In other words, some leading biologists of the time considered Wallace and Darwin's ideas were not a notable advance.

The fact that Darwin's narrative was speculative did not prevent it from becoming widespread. Publication of The Origin put the theory at the forefront of scientific thought. The idea quickly became closely linked with the name Charles Darwin. Unfortunately, history has treated Wallace as something akin to Darwin's assistant. Apparently, it is considered correct to attribute the theory to Darwin because his popular book had multiple examples and observations. According to this story, Wallace merely described the basic ideas.

Both Matthew and Wallace gave clear descriptions of natural selection. Nonetheless, throughout this book, I describe the theory as Darwin's, as is conventional. Still, it should be clear that he shares the credit.

## Credit and Context

Darwin's theory of evolution came about in a world changing from Jane Austin's Pride and Prejudice to the Victorian world of Charles Dickens. England was rapidly moving from genteel coaches and sailing ships to the railways and iron ships of Isambard Kingdom Brunel. In addition, the nobility and church were under threat from the influence of rich industrialists with a new scientific and business outlook. Moreover, Charles Darwin belonged to an extraordinarily influential and prosperous family. Furthermore, he had married his wealthy cousin Emma Wedgwood of the famous pottery company.

Darwin was a gentleman with a large house who never had to work. He was a part of the intellectual establishment and a Royal Society fellow at age 30. His famous voyage on the Beagle was what in modern terms might be described as an expensive adventure holiday rather than a job, an extended gap year perhaps. This

---

[63] Hussey A. (1859) Review, Zoologist, 17, 6474-6475.

description is not to minimise Darwin's contribution. Much of science arose from gentlemen with the time and funds to follow their interests in those days. However, we should contrast Darwin's position with Wallace, who earned his living as a middle-class specimen collector.

Wallace was born into a large middle-class family in Wales. Academically he was off to a poor start, and lack of funds forced him to leave grammar school to enter work at age 14. After many jobs, Wallace decided to combine his biology interests with work by going on an adventure. He went on an expedition to South America funded by collecting insects and other specimens. Wallace's return to England was dramatic. A fire on his ship took his vital specimens and left him to survive in an open boat. Fortunately, Wallace continued his collecting work and was in Borneo when the evolution papers were published. He was happy to be recognised as the joint originator of natural selection with Darwin, the great biologist. He seems to have quickly accepted that people would know the theory as Darwinism, but it had made his career.

There is no reason to suggest that either Darwin or Wallace had read Matthew's book or knew his work. It is conventional in science to assume honesty. Charles Darwin seems to have made efforts to attribute credit to other scientists. Despite this, the idea has arisen that Darwin and possibly Wallace cheated by not referring to Matthew being the originator of natural selection.[64] This accusation is unfair.

Curiously, Darwin wrote to Charles Lyell about Matthew's book. "I have ordered the book, as some few passages are rather obscure but it, is, certainly, I think, a complete but not developed anticipation!" We may forgive Darwin for being somewhat miffed. Still, the use of the word anticipation is odd. Matthew did not anticipate Darwin with natural selection; he had beaten him to the punch by a couple of decades. He suggests Matthew had not fully developed the idea, which presumably refers to the background narrative included in The Origin. Conversely, it would appear that Patrick Matthew considered Darwin's follow up obvious.

---

[64] Sutton M. (2017) Nullius in Verba: Darwin's Greatest Secret, CreateSpace.

Things are a little murkier, however. Darwin was clearly peeved by the idea that Matthew claimed credit for natural selection. In 1865, he wrote to his friend Hooker. "So poor old Patrick Matthew is not the first, and he cannot, or ought not to put on his title-pages 'Discover of Natural Selection'". Some may consider this a bit rich coming from a person who was famous for the same idea. Interestingly, Darwin was suggesting that some credit should be given to William Wells.

Wells was an American born physician and scientist. Darwin states that Wells "distinctly recognises the principle of natural selection, and this is the first recognition which has been indicated". Wells took the same approach as Darwin comparing artificial with natural selection. Unfortunately, Wells suggested that beneficial traits could not spread in a population. Also, Wells described the different human races, skin colour and related characteristics, which remains controversial.

It is claimed that Darwin was unaware of both Wells and Matthew before writing The Origin. This is reasonable, but he was aware of the work of another earlier evolutionist. Edward Blyth was an English born zoologist of limited means who mainly worked in India. Blythe had described the process of natural selection rather verbosely in papers on varieties.[65] Once again, Blyth was more concerned about maintaining a stable form rather than generating new species.

One puzzling aspect of Darwin was why he did not publish his ideas earlier. He clearly thought natural selection was of primary importance – his big idea. There are many explanations, such as he did not wish to upset his Christian wife. In addition, he was busy writing about other topics. Perhaps, he thought it a massive undertaking. So he was hoping to produce a complete account that would be immediately accepted. On the other hand, maybe he was not confident that he could formulate the idea well enough before receiving Wallace's paper. Still, Wallace and Matthew both managed to make brief, clear presentations.

---

[65] Eg: Blyth E. (1835) An attempt to classify the "varieties" of animals, with observations on the marked seasonal and other changes which naturally take place in various British species, and which do not constitute varieties, Magazine of Natural History, 8, 40–53; Blyth E. (1837) On the psychological distinctions between man and all other animals, Magazine of Natural History, 10, 131-141.

## Science as Narrative

Natural selection was a single explanation that biologists could apply to the whole of life. For some, it could be a fundamental law like those of Isaac Newton. In this sense, it is presented as a simple algorithm that dominates life. However, there are many algorithms used by living creatures.

The lowly ant uses interesting algorithms to aid decision making. Scientists investigating ants searching for food uncovered something exciting. Ants move out randomly from the nest. If they find food, they leave a chemical trail, allowing others to follow the path. The chemical slowly disperses in the air, fading with time. This is an efficient solution. Short routes and more ants collecting the food strengthen the chemical signal. When the food is exhausted, the ants stop depositing the chemical and continue their search. The method is simple, and it is the basis of ant algorithms in artificial intelligence.[66]

The ant algorithm explaining their search method was found by experiment and verified by replication. However, natural selection does not clarify evolution in the same way. It makes no predictions and is historical in its application looking back to explain what has already happened. It is not really a scientific theory, as it is not properly testable or refutable. Natural selection is more a belief system than an algorithm. All too often, natural selection is overused as an empty explanation.

Natural selection suffers from the narrative fallacy. How did the ants come up with the algorithm for finding food – natural selection. Why do ants use this particular algorithm – natural selection. How did ants get a brain to process the information – natural selection. Why are ants red – natural selection. Why did the red ants turn green – natural selection. What is the answer to the next question – natural selection. It is clearly absurd when overused in this way.

People like stories and find them convincing. In The Origin, Darwin supported his claims for natural selection with a series of narratives. Artificial breeding of animals such as dogs, cats, pigs, and chickens was a well-known worldwide activity. Moreover, farmers

---

[66] Dorigo M. *et al* (2006) Ant colony optimization: artificial ants as a computational intelligence technique, IEEE Computational Intelligence Magazine, 1(4), 28–39.

selectively bred crop plants for thousands of years. Breeding animals and plants was widespread; even a humble gardener might produce a new variety of rose.

Darwin described artificial selection where a pigeon fancier breeds diverse varieties of birds. Breeders produced these pigeons from a single species, the common rock dove (Columba livia). Those fanciers interested in a bird with a magnificent display of tail feathers, a fantail, would choose to breed birds with marked rear plumage. A similar selective breeding process might generate a new variety of pouter that impressively inflates its crop. Likewise, selecting the tendency to cartwheel over backwards in-flight might create a tumbler pigeon variety.

In animal and plant breeding, Darwin focussed on selection and argued that crossbreeding played little part. However, Darwin tried too hard to make his point and was a bit misleading. A later examination by geneticist Raymond Pearl found the opposite. He suggested, "Darwinian selection plays an extremely minor and unimportant part in the process as it is actually performed".[73]

Pearl's comment relates to breeding and crossbreeding and does not imply that selection is less critical in evolution. Still, the role of sexual selection in heredity may be more important than recognised.[67]

Darwin dealt with objections, such as dog breeders created a wide range from Pekinese to Great Danes. Still, they were all identifiably dogs and not new species. Darwin suggested that new species arose over a longer time scale. Even tiny changes might accumulate over millions of years and eventually lead to new species.

Darwin supported his claims with descriptions of variation in the wild; he was a superb naturalist with a gift for observation and explanation. He wove the known facts into stories linked by natural selection. It agreed with what biologists knew about plant and animal varieties. It seemed easy to understand and supported a social hierarchy based on merit. Importantly, it gave capitalists more power to challenge the dominance of the church and aristocracy. Darwin and his followers went further and claimed a central role for individual competition.

---

[67] Roughgarden J. (2009) The Genial Gene, Univ. California Press.

A close examination of Darwin's narrative shows its limitations. Future biologists could always provide a story. Creationists would later refer to these evolutionary tales as just-so stories referring to Rudyard Kipling's just so tales for children.[68] Kipling's imaginative tales include "How the Camel Got His Hump" and "How the Leopard Got His Spots". Leading biologists such as Stephen Jay Gould have made similar criticisms. He also questioned stories from sociobiology and evolutionary psychology that explain human behaviour by the evolution of genes. Gould did not believe these justifications were testable or scientific.

Gould used the giraffe's neck as a classic evolutionary just-so story.[69] A naive natural selection explanation is that the giraffe's ancestors with long necks found eating from higher in trees and bushes easier. This extra food would provide them with a survival advantage in times of shortage. Therefore, over time giraffes with genes for longer necks would be favoured. Seems reasonable. However, a little thought will show that the story is circular. Today's giraffes have long necks and can eat from high up in trees. Therefore, we can explain this by long-necked ancestors being selected for eating in this way. It is a weak and circular explanation. Great care should be taken when applying natural selection as a justification.

## Not So Gradual?

A classic evolutionary story concerned Galapagos finches. A big finch with a strong, wide beak can eat large nuts and seeds. The sturdy bill enables a bird to crack open tough shells but is clumsy for picking up and handling smaller seeds. By contrast, a different finch species with a delicate narrow beak eats smaller, softer nuts and seeds. These seeds accumulate in cracks and fissures and are out of reach of its hefty beaked competition. The result over time might explain the separation of the finches into two species.

In 1936, a hundred years after Darwin's trip to the Galapagos, Percy Lowe described them as Darwin's finches. Lowe claimed that they should be the leading focus of ornithologists because of their

---

[68] Kipling R. (2007) A Collection of Rudyard Kipling's Just So Stories, Walker Books.
[69] Olson M.E. Arroyo-Santos A. (2015) How to study adaptation, Quarterly Review of Biology, 90 (2), 167-191.

importance to evolution.[70] Biologist David Lack continued this research and considered the differences in bill size as breeding recognition signals. So, big beaked females might prefer large beaked males. Thus, the beaks serve as species isolating mechanisms.[71]

Lack emphasised that the differences in beak size are adaptations to specific food niches. Note that recognising and exploiting food niches depends on the birds' ability to observe, evaluate, and respond to signals. Following Lack's work, Ernst Mayer considered generating new species depends on isolating mechanisms that allow organisms to diverge.[72] In this case, living on islands and eating different food helped the species separate on the Galapagos.

Peter and Rosemary Grant and their students studied Darwin's finches in the Galapagos for over 40 years.[73] They confirmed that drought and rainfall on Daphne Major Island exerted selection pressure on the finch populations. Rapid changes in body and beak size occurred following changes in the food supply. As might be expected, weather-related food shortages devastated the population of finches in a single season.

In the early 1980s, El Niño brought prolonged rain followed by drought to Daphne Major. The plants responded to changes in the weather. The number of seeds went down through the dry period, and their size and hardness increased. As time passed, the smaller birds with the weakest beaks found it challenging to find food, and their numbers declined. The large beaked birds had a survival advantage as they could eat the larger tough seeds.

Surviving females chose the larger males with the deepest beaks for mating. Female mate choice varied with the conditions and helped drive the population change. When exceptionally heavy rains replaced the drought, the plants responded by producing smaller soft seeds. The tables had turned. Small beaked birds now had the advantage, and large beaked finches were short of food.

---

[70] Lowe P.R. (1936) The finches of the Galapagos in relation to Darwin's conception of species, April, A paper read before the British Association (1935 Darwin Centenary), https://doi.org/10.1111/j.1474-919X.1936.tb03376.
[71] Lack D. (1947) Darwin's Finches, Cambridge Univ. Press.
[72] Mayr E. (1985) The Growth of Biological Thought, Harvard Univ. Press.
[73] Weiner J. (1995) The Beak of the Finch, Vintage.

The Grant's measurements on the finches demonstrated that population change is a variable, dynamic process. Evolutionary stress can vary from season to season or even from day to day. Fortunately, they studied the island during extreme rain and drought that caused the birds to suffer intense survival pressure. As a result, it was clear that natural selection could cause rapid population change. As expected, environmental stress can reduce the size of a population in a short period. Notably, the things that make a bird fit in drought could be unfavourable in wet periods.

The Grant's had shown that microevolution was an active process, and change could occur rapidly. However, this is limited in scope. These minor variations do not necessarily apply to macroevolution. Therefore, it does not directly explain significant species change, such as generating the first frog or howler monkey.[74] Unfortunately, there is currently no way to check for long-term gradual species change experimentally. The geological time scales prevent direct observation. Tracking history with the geological record or DNA reveals change over time but does not indicate the cause.

## Darwin's Smart Organisms

Notice throughout that the finch studies describe intelligent behaviour. Small beaked birds recognise they have delicate little bills, and they concentrate on finding and eating small seeds. Eating suitable seeds may be innate or learned by trial and error when manipulating and cracking seeds. Also, the female birds recognised fitter males, and their choice influenced mating and thus future generations. Fitness and survival depend on decision-making.

## Neutral Selection

What happens when fitness is removed from natural selection? The neutral selection theory approach assumes the evolutionary change is just chance.[75] Neutral selection is random change. Thus, mutations are neutral rather than beneficial or harmful. At first, this seems extreme, but it helps sort out what fitness means.

---

[74] Rapid speciation is possible by aneuploidy or a change in the number of chromosomes.
[75] Leigh E.G. (2007) Neutral theory: a historical perspective, J. Evol. Biol., 20(6), 2075-2091.

Chance leads to differences between successive populations. Over an extended period, the population drifts about randomly. Small groups are most susceptible to this random drift. Drift could result in more Darwin's finches having fat beaks over time as chance eliminates thin beaks. Despite being just accidental, it might appear that some factor had favoured the fat beaked birds. An observer might wrongly conclude that the fat beaked birds were fitter and had a higher likelihood of survival. The apparent fitness would be an illusion.

There is a well-known story of a financier who employed 100 market traders. He gave them a budget and set them off to see who could make money. At the end of the first trial period, he sacked half of the traders who made the least profit or, even worse, made a loss. The trial continued. At the end of the second trial period, he again sacked half of the remaining 50 traders who performed least well. The financier carried on selecting the best until he had only one trader left.

The financier thought he had found the cleverest, most successful trader. However, if the market were random, it would still produce a spread of profits and losses. He would still end up with a single apparently successful trader. If they were winning or losing at random, the selected trader was just lucky. There was no talent involved. Just as a gambler winning at roulette does not mean his play was skilful.

Neutral evolution often does not model life well. It has applications in molecular evolution but is less helpful for living organisms. One of the problems is the results meander about in a random walk. It produces change over time, but it is slow and inefficient. There is no directionality to the process. In reality, many mutations are harmful, and a few can even be beneficial. A natural modification, the nearly neutral theory, includes some mutations that are not neutral.[76] Introducing harmful or beneficial mutations provides an improved driver for change and takes us back to fitness.

---

[76] Ohta T. (1973) Slightly deleterious mutant substitutions in evolution, Nature, 246(5428), 96-98.

If we continue with our machine intelligence analogy, there are supervised and unsupervised techniques. We discussed this earlier with Dawkins' simple computer model. Supervised is when the process is given a target. The engineer does not provide a target for an unsupervised machine. Instead, it tries to find one of its own, but finding a target can be demanding. Supervised methods are generally easier to implement, faster, and more effective.

Now a target indicates a local aim rather than evolution producing ever-improving organisms. Life does not have an overall direction. However, a target speeds up beneficial change.

## Natural Selection

Natural selection is not what most people believe it is. Biologists use the term as an umbrella explanation that they can apply to any evolutionary change. For some biologists, it explains everything; evolution is natural selection. Darwin encouraged this view while Wallace considered there were limits.

Natural selection is sometimes presented with the role of fitness buried and ignored. A varied population contains some animals that are more likely to survive and have children. The next generation includes more of their offspring. This uses variation and selection to get around the issue of fitness and makes the process seem automatic. It looks like a simple physical process.

The first thing to notice is that this approach to natural selection is just accounting for differences in successive generations. By accounting, I mean a bookkeepers view. Say the parent generation of finches contains 70% with fat beaks and 30% with pointy beaks. The following generation has 71% fat beaks and only 29% sharp beaks. The birds were selected in some way. Suppose this process were to continue for multiple generations. In that case, the change could be significant enough to form a population of only big beaked birds. However, this just says a considerable shift can occur in many little steps.

Natural selection is bookkeeping.

Taken alone, such accounting has no explanatory power. It does not provide a causative explanation, merely bookkeeping. Selection is not an answer in itself. Natural selection as an explanation needs fitness. Fitness and risk cause change, which the selection numbers report.

## Fitness

As the name suggests, engineers use evolutionary algorithms modelled on biological change. Some computer scientists model fitness as the chance an individual will leave offspring in the next generation.[77] Unfortunately, this hints that fitness is a result of the selection rather than its cause.

The basic approach is close to Darwin's original idea of natural selection and shows its limitations. One of the simplest algorithms selects the more favoured outcome from a random population and removes individuals who don't come up to scratch. With each generation, there is some loss of variety, and engineers add more random variation. Gradually over time, the result is a population with something like the required outcome. I say 'something like' because these Monte-Carlo style methods are not particularly powerful. As algorithms go, the approach is easy to understand, easy to implement, and weak.

As expected, engineers find that increasing the number of random points gives a better result. This improvement is the case with many machine intelligence techniques. However, no matter how many data points are used, simple selection is a weak method. Furthermore, adding more data or more generations does not necessarily overcome the limitations. I mention this here because of Darwin's use of gradualism. In Darwin's view, the slight difference between generations did not matter because of the millions of years over which nature generated new species. Thus, it appears that Darwin overestimated the benefits of increased time on simple selection.

However, there are many evolutionary algorithms in AI. One approach of particular interest is the use of genetic algorithms modelled on Neo-Darwinism. This method includes sex. Many animals and plants engage in sexual reproduction. One reason for sex is to share genetic information and spread variety in the population.

---

[77] Eg: Maynard Smith J. (1998) Evolutionary Genetics, Oxford.

Sexual reproduction randomly mixes and shares the chromosomes. Chromosomes are tiny cell components consisting of DNA and protein. Human cells generally have 46 chromosomes in 23 pairs. These pairs are reduced to singles, one from each pair, in the sperm and egg. The father donates one set of 23, and each pairs up with the corresponding chromosome in the mother's egg. So the offspring receives randomly selected chromosomes, half from the father and half from the mother.

The jumbled selection of chromosomes is supplemented with DNA crossover. Within the chromosome is a length of DNA. During sexual reproduction, the DNA may crossover and re-join somewhere along the DNA chain's length. So the offspring now receives chromosomes containing mixed genes and is a genetically unique individual. Computer scientists include sexual reproduction in genetic algorithms by simulating crossover.

Genetic algorithms are an interesting general optimisation method for machine intelligence. These algorithms have a population of software organisms with virtual genes contained in chromosomes. The genes are randomly mutated to add variety. Chromosomes can crossover when organisms have virtual sex and produce the next generation. A fitness function culls the population at each generation.

Genetic algorithms are not that powerful.

Still, genetic algorithms have some properties that should disturb evolutionary biologists. Genetic algorithms do not have the ultimate problem-solving abilities that some Neo-Darwinists ascribe to natural selection acting on genes. Genetic algorithm optimisation is slow, and the starting conditions constrain the result. Nevertheless, like Neo-Darwinism, genetic algorithms are powerful enough to explain how breeders generate dog varieties. Still, to continue the analogy, they would not turn a dog into a cat.

Some years ago, I was researching genetic algorithms to design and structure neural networks. I suppose the media description might be I was evolving an electronic brain. Unfortunately, the genetic algorithms were slow at optimisation. Moreover, the resulting neural networks were not particularly quick at learning and not that accurate. Increasing the number of generations or the size of the evolving population was not rewarding. In the end, I was able to optimise the neural networks quickly using an alternative approach. Modelling the neural network on brain development rather than evolution resulted in fast, efficient networks that were far more capable and useful.

AI and machine intelligence can model natural selection, but evolutionary algorithms are not particularly special as techniques go. Each approach to machine intelligence has its strengths and weaknesses. Engineers choose the method or combination that is most likely to be helpful for a particular application. Moreover, genetic algorithms depend critically on how the programmer includes fitness. Biologists who praise the fantastic properties of natural selection and genetics might usefully spend a little more time trying their evolutionary ideas on a computer.

## Cause and Effect

Some biologists have long claimed that natural selection is the cause of evolution. But what does the selection? Non-random selection needs a cause that comes before the effect. The standard answer is the environment, competition, predation, disease, and so on. We can shorten this to it is the environment that causes the selection. However, this is also incomplete. The environment has a propensity for selecting organisms – it removes those that are least fit and able to adapt.

*Fitness is to natural selection as cause is to effect.*

Fitness for the environment is the critical element of evolution. It is the driving factor. A fox will kill rabbits, but the animals it kills are those least able to avoid it. Selection is the result of both fitness and chance in determining the survival and reproduction of an individual. In real life, it is clear that not all animals are equally able to survive. Some will be able to run faster and evade predators. Others will have more body fat and be slower but more able to resist starvation. It is thus not obvious what form fitness takes at a particular time. In one case, a mouse avoids predators, and in another, it dies of hunger. The stresses on a population vary with weather, location, and so on.

Behaviour drives fitness, which determines the result of natural selection. The issue of fitness is the primary concern with trying to use natural selection to explain evolution. Indeed, we could forget the phrase natural selection and consider just fitness for the environment. In short, the mechanism driving natural selection is well described as the survival of the fittest – a phrase that hints at an underlying cause. Considering fitness alone gives an identical result to natural selection. In this view, the selection is just the outcome, accounting for the effect of fitness in the particular environment.

We can redefine fitness as the ability of the organism to adapt. Adaptation is an organism's behaviour that makes it better suited to survive and reproduce in an environment. So now we have a dynamic process, and natural selection starts to make sense as an explanation.

Natural selection is an outcome rather than a cause.

The current framework for adaptation is that natural selection makes an organism able to live in its habitat. Evolutionary adaptation is supposedly inherited, making learning, flexibility, and physiological change a result of genetics. The gene is said to be the evolutionary replicator providing long-term stability and control.[114] By contrast, adaptation is dynamic and depends on the ability to compute.

There is a species that clearly changed its evolution by decision-making. The first Homo sapiens skeletal remains are from about 300,000 years ago. Neanderthals came before Homo sapiens and were already wearing clothes. Before that were Homo erectus, they invented fire, cooking, and moved out of Africa. Long before that, there was Homo habilis and even earlier Australopithecus with stone tools. Agriculture alone had a massive influence on subsequent human development. Throughout human history, offspring were getting ideas from their parents or by observing others.

Humans made the modern environment; people have transformed their survival pressures with science, technology, and medicine. Early humans discovered and used fire, which altered all subsequent generations and influenced their future evolution. Still, other organisms influence their survival with intelligent behaviour and tool use. For example, scientists recently found birds in Australia spreading wildfires by taking burning sticks to other locations.[78]

---

[78] Bonita M. *et al* (2017), Intentional fire-Spreading by "Firehawk" raptors in Northern Australia, J. of Ethnobiology, 37(4), 700-718.

Firehawks move fire up to a kilometre to a more convenient place for hunting the displaced and cooked fauna. But, once again, humility is necessary. The Aborigines apparently knew about the firebirds, which were part of their culture and history. Anthropologists assumed the natives' story of the crow that stole the secret of fire was just a myth.

Other animals are at the stage of rudimentary tool use and language. In the 1970s, tool use was supposed to separate intelligent man from dumb animals.[79] But, unfortunately, biologists only saw what they wanted. So, unexpectedly, tool use is surprisingly frequent in the animal kingdom. A puffin might use a twig to scratch an itch.[80] A chimp uses a stick to get ants from their nest[81] or perhaps for hunting or fishing.[82] Beavers dam rivers. Ants create bridges. Birds build complicated nests. Spiders weave intricate geometric webs. Look about. Lots of animals use tools.

Then there was the human use of language – but you can train a chimp to communicate.[83] Kanzi, the bonobo, understood spoken English and could talk using a modified keyboard. When objectors claimed Washoe the chimp was just using symbols rather than actual language. The response was to teach another chimp, Nim Chimpsky, sign language.[84] Despite the name, Nim Chimpsky is only distantly related to that other primate Noam Chomsky. Chimps might not have the language facility of a modern human, but they can understand and converse. Besides, ants, bees, and even single cells communicate; as Darwin claimed, the human difference is one of degree.

## Woodpeckers

Returning to Darwin's finches, there are said to be about 18 species in the Galapagos Islands.[85] One species stands out. The

[79] Oakley K.P. (1972) Man the Tool-Maker, British Museum (Natural History).
[80] Fayet A.L. *et al* (2020) Evidence of tool use in a seabird, PNAS, 117(3), 1277-1279.
[81] Sugiyama Y. (1995) Tool-use for catching ants by chimpanzees at Bossou and Monts Nimba, West Africa, Primates 36, 193–205.
[82] Pruetz J.D. *et al* (2015) New evidence on the tool-assisted hunting exhibited by chimpanzees (Pan troglodytes verus) in a savannah habitat at Fongoli, Sénégal, Royal Society Open Science, 2(4), 140507.
[83] Savage–Rumbaugh S. Lewin R. (1994) Kanzi, Wiley.
[84] Terrace H.S. (1979) Nim: A Chimpanzee Who Learned Sign Language, Knopf.

woodpecker finch eats seeds like the other birds but specialises in invertebrates, insects, and grubs. These finches have developed tool use. They employ twigs and cactus spines to winkle out grubs from crevices.[86]

These smart birds[87] can adapt and learn. Notably, woodpecker finches vary their tool use depending on the circumstances, and some birds don't use them. The finches make their tools out of any suitable available material and use the same tool repeatedly. They will shorten them as needed or select a longer stick to get at a grub in a deep crevice. Also, it appears that young woodpecker finches can learn tool use by trial and error and do not need to be taught the technology by others.[88]

Biologists suggested that the Galapagos woodpecker finch took to using tools because it has a short tongue. Animals searching crevices for insects often evolve a long sticky tongue. For example, true woodpeckers have strong beaks, long tongues, and other physical adaptations. The Galapagos does not have true woodpeckers. So this was an opportunity, a finch could move into that niche using sticks to replace the long tongue.

Biologists thus claim that the absence of a real woodpecker and the harsh conditions on the Galapagos caused the finches to adopt tools. Some suggest that had a true woodpecker been present, the finch would not have been able to fill the niche.[89] However, it could equally be that the woodpecker finch's technology is more adaptable than a long sticky tongue.

A short tongue is not a mechanism that explains tool use. Such stories cannot remove the need for cognition. The woodpecker finch was motivated to develop tools because it found an available food supply, the grubs and insects. More likely, this is an example of speciation driven by behaviour. The bird appreciated a source of

[85] Grant P.R. Grant B. R. (2008) How And Why Species Multiply, Princeton Univ. Press

[86] Tebbich S. et al (2012) Use of a barbed tool by an adult and a juvenile woodpecker finch (Cactospiza pallida), Behavioural Processes, 89(2), 166-171.

[87] Tebbich S. Bshary R. (2004) Cognitive abilities related to tool use in the woodpecker finch, Cactospiza pallida, Animal Behaviour, 67(4), 689-697.

[88] Tebbich S. et al (2001) Do woodpecker finches acquire tool-use by social learning? Proc. Biol. Sci., 268(1482), 2189–2193.

[89] Van Driesche J. Van Driesche R. (2004) Nature Out of Place, Island Press.

food and found an alternative technology for hunting insects. Their decision to use tools increased their ability to survive, ultimately generating a new species.

## Sexual Selection

Darwin suggested an extension of natural selection in his 1871 book The Descent of Man.[90] Sexual selection is an animal choosing a mate based on visual appearance, behaviour, or other physical traits. An animal well endowed with the valued feature, say a peacock with impressive tail feathers, will find it easier to find mates and leave offspring. The male peacock's penalty is that his large and colourful tail feathers make him an easier target for predators.

Sexual preference is evident in humans, where males notably find several features of the female human anatomy desirable. However, other animals demonstrate similar sex attraction. Sexual adornment in birds is particularly apparent. However, mice, monkeys, dogs, and even fruit flies have shown sexual selection in experiments. In most cases, the male competes for the attention of the female. Darwin's view of sexual selection was aesthetic: "the taste for the beautiful". Perhaps here it is worth mentioning the beauty of butterflies. Like Darwin, the heretic within us might ask to what extent butterflies have aesthetic preferences.

Female choice often drives sexual selection. The females have a preference and judge the relative value of the male traits. For successful mating, the animals must recognise members of their own species. Equally, they separate males from females and appreciate the sex to which they belong. Then the animals signal and receive information for a compelling enticement. Almost by definition, communication and processing lead to decisions critical to reproduction. Sexual selection is smart behaviour dependent on signalling, communication, and above all, data processing.

Darwin was pointing out that reproductive behaviour could dominate natural selection. As in the peacock, the benefits of sexual selection can outweigh the risk of predation. In other words, a male

---

[90] Darwin C. (2019) The Descent of Man, Wentworth.

that is amazingly fit in the struggle for existence remains an evolutionary failure unless he can find a mate and leave offspring.

Some biologists disliked Darwin's view of sexual selection, which they attacked or ignored for a century. Sexual selection came back into popularity towards the end of the 20th century but without Darwin's aesthetics. Biologists could avoid aesthetics by assuming natural selection applied to mating preferences.[91] Notably, statistician Ronald Fisher suggested that genes for mate preference would link to those for display. The offspring would associate the male's display genes with those for female choice. The result would thus be self-reinforcing.[92] Fisher's idea might work provided genes caused the behaviour, in some as yet unknown way. Of course, Fisher knew little about computing and did not address how genes could control preferences and choice.

Alfred Wallace's views differed from those of Darwin. Wallace thought that sexual selection was a minor consideration and objected to the idea of aesthetics. The male ornamentation is often entirely separate from the best solution for survival. He considered decoration as a way of signalling vigour and health. Wallace pointed out that many internal organs such as the spleen and liver are quite brightly coloured and not part of a display.

Wallace doubted that a beetle or a butterfly could have sufficient aesthetic appreciation of its mate. His doubt was justified at the time. However, we can use our test of how difficult would it be to simulate the attraction with a robot. Let's take a robot butterfly with a simple learning computer and vision system. Our robot butterfly could learn to recognise either a form of beauty or apparent vigour. Indeed, there could be substantial overlap in the preferred signals, such as youth, symmetry, colour, and so on. Of course, the robot butterfly might not have the aesthetic appreciation of a human artist. Still, it could be adequate for reproductive choice.

Flowers provide a standard of aesthetic beauty for humans. Nevertheless, the flower is aiming to attract bees and other

---

[91] Prum R.O. (2012) Aesthetic evolution by mate choice: Darwin's really dangerous idea, Phil. Trans. R. Soc. B, 367, 2253–2265.
[92] Fisher R. A. (1915) The evolution of sexual preference, Eugen. Rev., 7, 184–191.

pollinating insects rather than humans. These insects have a nervous system and prefer the display. It is not just accidental that flowers are beautiful and smell nice. Ornithologist Richard Prum put it well. The design of a flower "is not determined by adaptation to mere physical challenges, but by the…sensory evaluations, consequent cognitive states, and economic decisions of…pollinators". Biologists would do well to consider flowers and their beauty in terms of the nervous systems they evolved to attract.

"You insist that there is something a machine cannot do. If you tell me precisely what it is a machine cannot do, then I can always make a machine which will do just that".

John von Neumann

# Sociopaths or Symbiosis?

"Psychopaths view any social exchange as a 'feeding opportunity,' a contest or a test of wills in which there can be only one winner. Their motives are to manipulate and take, ruthlessly and without remorse".

Robert Hare

Self-interest is exciting for some but using it universally in Neo-Darwinism was wrong-headed. It biased everything that followed. Evolutionists ignored Darwin's portrayals of love and empathy. Instead, they insisted on constructing evolution on a philosophy of animal psychopathy and self-interest. This inclination had widespread appeal and fitted the spirit of the age.

History has misinterpreted Darwin. He elaborated on the theory of evolution as "One general law, leading to the advancement of all organic beings, namely, multiply, vary, let the strongest live and the weakest die". This Darwin qualified with "In the long history of humankind (and animal kind, too) those who learned to collaborate and improvise most effectively have prevailed". While stressing the importance of competition, Darwin balanced it with cooperative mechanisms and adaptation. His words, "Besides love and sympathy, animals exhibit other qualities connected with the social instincts which in us would be called moral". This expression of animal empathy is far from the biology of ruthlessness popular with some of Darwin's followers.

Darwin's approach reflected his position in Victorian society. His ideas of fitness supported the values of merit and inherited privilege. Life is not fair. Top people were the best because they were born that way, and they deserved their place in the world. Britain led the industrial revolution but was in danger of sinking into a debased form of oligarchy. So it is hardly surprising that the new industrialists and power makers would welcome ideas of merit and hereditary fitness. Natural selection could be highly reassuring for those in a position of power or authority.

Darwin made people aware of natural selection at a time of social and technological upheaval. Some cold-blooded and influential people were happy to take on board the survival of the fittest as justification. Human races could have differing merit, which endorsed the need for Britain's empire. It gave respectability to those supporting eugenics, hoping to improve humans by selective breeding.

Fortunately, Darwin's publication followed the 1807 parliamentary act to abolish the transatlantic slave trade, which took effect in 1834. Slaves in the Caribbean gained freedom, but their release in some other British territories took longer. Former slaves were still forced to work for a low wage. Still, abolition was to some extent effective 20 years before The Origin. The Royal Navy had ended the slave trade. By the time of Darwin's Origin, the British West Africa Squadron had been interdicting slave ships for more than 50 years.

Darwin was a man of his time and held many of the Victorian political and philosophical views. In modern terms, he might be described as sexist and racist.[93] The subtitle of The Origin, "the preservation of favoured races in the struggle for life", is a giveaway. There was a gradation of humans, with white Europeans being favoured for intellect and achievement. Women were less capable and had smaller brains. He wrote that Europeans would eventually squeeze out savages, a term used for many indigenous peoples. Those who doubt this claim can simply read his other well-known book, The Descent of Man. It includes lines like "the civilised races of man will almost certainly exterminate and replace throughout the world the savage races". Alfred Wallace was less biased, and this was another source of friction between him and Darwin.

## Disordered Minds

Here we need to consider something often hidden from the historical discussion. We shall approach this delicate subject a little tangentially. The current psychiatric manuals describe a range of

---

[93] Rose S. (2009) Darwin, race and gender, EMBO Rep., 10(4), 297–298.

personality disorders.[94] These cover what some psychologists call sociopathy, psychopathy, and narcissism.[95] The popular idea of a psychopath is a deranged serial killer. It is probably the case that most serial killers are psychopaths; however, few psychopaths are serial killers. Most clever psychopaths live seemingly ordinary law-abiding lives.

We might expect this appearance of normality as a psychopath is just a person born without a conscience and lacking empathy. Importantly, psychopaths can be adept at hiding their personality traits. Some people are more self-interested, less kind and empathic than others, and there is a personality spectrum. Psychopaths are just outliers. About 1% of males and a smaller number of females have this extreme personality.

Psychopaths think being nice is dumb; of course, it's rational to look after yourself and fun to screw others over. Unfortunately, some will be unable to conceive of other possibilities. Why help others if it does not have a payoff for you? There is little difference between the viewpoint of the psychopath and biology as nature red in tooth and claw. In both cases, someone with a profound lack of empathy may be incapable of understanding cooperation and altruism.

Sociopaths are less extreme but more common, making up about 4% of people.[96] Sociopaths learn more of their behaviour rather than it being innate. A typical large class in school would have a person at this end of the personality spectrum; the class bully perhaps, or the person copying homework, sucking up to the teacher, and blaming others. Narcissists are a related group with overlapping traits; they have exaggerated feelings of self-importance and an extreme desire for admiration.

There is some dispute as to whether psychopathy is a psychiatric or a legal problem.[97] A psychopath is not sick in the usual meaning of the word. As is clear from fictional stories, prisons have a higher

[94] Kupfer D. Regier D. (2013) Diagnostic and Statistical Manual of Mental Disorders, Fifth Edition (DSM-5), American Psychiatric Association.
[95] Hare R. (1999) Without Conscience, Gilford Press.
[96] Stout M. (2006) The Sociopath Next Door, Broadway.
[97] Kaylor L. (1999) Antisocial personality disorder: diagnostic, ethical and treatment issues, Issues Ment. Health Nurs., 20(3), 247-258.

proportion of psychopaths than the general population. But so do many well-respected professions.[98]

Time magazines top 10 occupations with the highest proportion of psychopaths is telling. The list is CEO, lawyer, media (TV/Radio), salesperson, surgeon, journalist, police officer, clergyperson, chef, civil servant.[99] Perhaps not surprisingly, care assistant and nurse are amongst the jobs that attract the fewest. Also of interest are the clinical signs, which include criminal and antisocial behaviour. This odd inclusion of criminality eliminates professional people who might otherwise be labelled, such as the psychiatrists making the diagnosis. What is of interest is that politicians did not appear in these top tens.

Throughout history, politicians and leaders of countries have caused wars and other havoc. Many such leaders are described as psychopaths,[100] including Leopold 2$^{nd}$ of Belgium, Ivan the Terrible, Caligula, and Attila the Hun. More modern examples include Stalin, Hitler, Pol Pot, Idi Amin, Mou Zedong, and Saddam Hussain. History describes how psychopathic leaders have been responsible for aggressive war, genocide, and tyranny. Several well-known current politicians could meet the definition, and the reason for this is not hard to explain.

The characteristics of a successful politician are similar to those of narcissism and psychopathy. A strong leader should be charismatic, decisive, determined, exude confidence, be immune to criticism, and pass any blame on to others. Importantly, they need a facility for barefaced lying. While a stupid psychopath can end up serving multiple prison sentences, a bright example might well be running the country. Any country.

People with psychopathic tendencies may be particularly attracted to a description of nature as a competitive world lacking empathy. A world in which an organism will track, hunt, and kill to survive. Following the old proverb, all's fair in love and war, and all life is

[98] Babiak P. Hare R.D. (2009) Snakes in Suits, Harper Collins.
[99] Barker E. (2014) Which professions have the most psychopaths? The fewest? March 21, Time.com, accessed, Jan 2020; Dodgson L. (2018) The 10 professions with the most psychopaths, May 20, Businessinsider.com, accessed Jan 2020.
[100] Lobaczewski A.M. Knight-Jadczyk L. (2012) Political Ponerology, Red Pill Press.

love and war. Psychopathy does have advantages in situations that reward a high tolerance for risk and ruthless behaviour.[101] Fighter pilots, special forces soldiers, and financial decision-makers are examples of activities where some psychopaths can thrive. Like many other fictional heroes, James Bond displays psychopathic tendencies.

Conversely, there is an anecdote about Inuit psychopaths. Throughout the world, psychopaths seem to make up a consistent but small number of the population. So there may have been an evolutionary imperative for human groups to have a small proportion of 'leaders' and a majority of 'followers'.[102] However, some Inuits and other arctic groups claimed not to have such people. When pressed, they responded that such people went for a walk on the ice and did not return. Inuits living in a severe and threatening environment would not tolerate destructive people.

Unfortunately, voters tend to vote for so-called strong leaders with psychopathic and narcissistic personalities. Managers will choose them in interviews, and surprisingly parole boards preferentially release them. However, despite their manipulation, appeal, and charisma, a standard heuristic for dealing with sociopaths and narcissists is: get away and stay away. Because, in general, they are bad news. They cause a great deal more harm than good.

## Preconceived Notions

Those of the more sociopathic tendencies can turn science into a belief system. Science is never settled or a result of consensus. It is an active and open process. However, for many, once an idea has taken hold, it is difficult to shift.

The classic example from physics is of two seemingly conflicting theories of light. There were two beliefs; light is particles or light is waves. If you believed light is waves, you could design multiple experiments to show this was so. The results would confirm your prejudice. However, believe in light as particles, and your experiments demonstrate that is the case. Eventually, physicists realised that both ideas were correct. Light is made of photons or particles with a wavelength. The conflicting results depended on how

[101] Dutton K. (2013) The Wisdom of Psychopaths, Arrow.
[102] Koestler A. (1978) Janus: A Summing Up, Random House.

the scientist designed their experiment. The combined theory, quantum mechanics, is weird and full of apparent contradictions. It is, however, the most successful theory in physics. Besides, contradictions thrill scientists. As Isaac Asimov put it, "The most exciting phrase to hear in science, the one that heralds new discoveries, is not, 'Eureka! I've found it,' but, 'That's funny!'"

## Belief

Natural selection is a possible and plausible description of evolution's history. However, stretch natural selection to cover all evolution, and it becomes a form of faith. It explains everything and nothing.

Some Neo-Darwinians act as if biology is a belief system and use it to attack religion.[103] Richard Dawkins represents a particular and extreme view of Neo-Darwinian evolution. Dawkins promotion of selfish gene ideas has ended up with a belief system based on the omnipotence of natural selection. The popularity of Dawkins and other rampant atheists means we need to address their 'god question' here. This silly evolution vs genesis argument has been a distraction ever since Darwin published The Origin. We need to remove this level of banality.

In many cases, people find the idea of evolution acceptable but baulk at natural selection as a complete explanation. Much of this rejection can be placed at the altar of the atheists who have long insisted that evolution disproves religion, somehow. Does science really need this lowbrow nonsense? The scope of science is limited and tells us little, if anything, about religious belief. To repeat, science depends on experiments, and there is no experiment to test the existence of God. So decide for yourself what you believe. Whatever your answer, put it to one side and take an open-minded approach to real science. Biology and religion are absolutely separate.

Amusingly, both Neo-Darwinian atheists and the religious argue that humans are unique. The bible suggests that humans are extraordinary creatures made in the image of God. Some biology driven atheists seem to agree and defend their shared ideas with a

---

[103] Eg: Dawkins R. (2006) The God Delusion, Black Swan.

similar zeal. Amusingly, I have met Neo-Darwinists and others who reject faith but talk about living in a computer simulation.[104] These atheists appear to miss the similarity between an ultimate programmer and a deity. There is no ultimate designer in science.

For decades, some evolutionary biologists have been glorifying the internal consistency of Neo-Darwinian ideas. Unfortunately, this incestuous approach has been bad news for biology. Instead of assuming all life is psychopathic, they need to embrace other possibilities. The main challenger is the opposite idea, symbiosis.

## Lichens

Lichens are the poster child for symbiosis. Life can produce astonishingly complex and intelligent symbiotic organisms. These creatures are adapted and smart in their environment but not in others. Notably, a typical symbiotic organism is involved in multiple collaborations.

Scientists estimate that lichens cover a surprising amount of the earth, growing on almost any terrestrial surface. There are perhaps 20,000 species, and they tolerate extreme environments, from deserts to the arctic tundra. Nevertheless, they are typically plain and often overlooked. They are usually slow-growing and some of the oldest living organisms.

Lichens appear like dull plants. They vary greatly, looking like anything from a powdery deposit, or crusty leaves, to a mini-shrub. A lichen gives the appearance of being just another plant species. That is, it looks and acts like a single organism.

Lichens can be considered single organisms or societies. They are colonies of cooperating species and contain at least one fungus and one or more photosynthetic organisms. Algae or cyanobacteria produce energy from sunlight and share it with the fungi. In return, the fungi give the lichen its structure and provide minerals and shelter. The fungi in lichens are varied and not closely related, having evolved separately. Their photosynthetic partners are similarly diverse. It is becoming apparent that the lichen symbiosis may often

---

[104] Moskowitz C. (2016) Are we living in a computer simulation? Scientific American, Apr. 7.

involve more organisms, including yeasts and bacteria. Such cooperation is not limited to lichens but is ever-present in biology.

## Symbiosis

Selfish gene ideas have concealed some of the most outstanding biological developments that arise from symbiosis. Both cooperation and competition are necessary for successful evolution. Smart organisms are not so limited, as they behave selfishly or altruistically according to their current strategy.

Although not generally acknowledged, Neo-Darwinism has fundamental limitations. For example, many assume that genetics explains heredity, all heredity. The presumption is partly correct as genes contain the information needed to produce proteins. However, while proteins are essential, they do not uniquely create an organism's structure, behaviour or drive evolution. We have a somewhat more plausible mechanism when we add control genes that switch other genes ON or OFF.

Lynn Margulis argued that some of the most remarkable developments in evolution involve symbiosis rather than Neo-Darwinism. She described how cells with nuclei developed as colonies. These large eukaryotic cells form plants, animals, fungi, and complex microorganisms. The creatures and the life we see about us are made of eukaryotic cells.

The formation of eukaryotic cells may be the single most dramatic and vital step in life's history.[105] Lynn Margulis revived the symbiosis idea from Russian biologist Konstantin Mereschkowski. Over a century ago, Mereschkowski described how eukaryotic cells might have formed. Eukaryotic cells typically contain hundreds of particles called mitochondria from which they obtain most of their energy. Mitochondria also play a significant part in the control of the cell's biochemistry and behaviour.

Margulis described how mitochondria came from bacteria taken into the body of a larger cell. The large cell absorbed a bacterium, and both cells found the result extremely beneficial. Bacteria provided the big cell with an increase in energy and efficiency. In

---

[105] Mayr E. (2001) What Evolution Is, Basic Books.

return, the large cell provided a safe, protected environment for the bacteria. It was a win-win solution.

Another win-win solution of symbiosis is the incorporation of chloroplasts by plant cells. Chloroplasts give leaves their green colour and convert sunlight and carbon dioxide into usable energy. Margulis explained that chloroplasts were cyanobacteria absorbed by a larger cell. Once again, it was mutually beneficial; the chloroplast provided energy in return for a stable environment.

Notice that Lynn Margulis had turned the idea of evolution by competition, the survival of the fittest if you like, into progress by cooperation. Her vision was anathema to Richard Dawkins and similar biologists who believed in ruthless competition. It refuted their belief system. So Dawkins and others discounted Margulis's ideas. Indeed, she could not even get her papers published. Peer-reviewed journals just rejected the idea outright. Peer review censorship is a waste of time and effort for scientists who challenge the prevailing dogma. In Margulis's case, she submitted a version of her original paper on symbiosis[106] to around 15 journals before one accepted it for publication.

However, Dawkins did ultimately admit she was right. He later described it as "one of the great achievements of twentieth-century evolutionary biology".[107] Looking back, it is difficult to comprehend why some biologists had such a problem with Margulis and symbiosis. Cells merge, and such fusion is commonplace. Heart, muscle, and stem cells fuse together.[108] Such cell fusion occurred billions of times throughout evolution. A critical example is a fusion between cancer and white blood cells, which is a common strategy complicating treatment.[109] If the resulting symbiotic cooperation gave some advantage, then Darwinian selection would ensure its survival and prosperity.

Lynn Margulis explained how the cells' decision to work together and form a new organism specified how future evolution would

---

[106] Sagan L. (1967) On the origin of mitosing cells, J. Theor. Biol., 14(3), 255-274.
[107] Brockman J. (1995) The Third Culture, Simon & Schuster.
[108] Eg: Reinecke H. *et al* (2004) Evidence for fusion between cardiac and skeletal muscle cells, Circulation Research, 94, e56–e60.
[109] Eg: Weiler J. Dittmar T. (2019) Cell fusion in human cancer, Cells, 8(2), 132.

proceed. The combined cells forced the genes to adapt to the new conditions. Mutations occurred in the mitochondrial DNA, and some genes moved to the cell nucleus. This gene movement locked in the symbiosis. The changed controls avoid the mitochondria switching back to life as independent bacteria. The eukaryotic cell is a system with all its parts working together.

## Gaia

Lynn Margulis went on to work on Gaia with James Lovelock. Gaia is the idea that living organisms maintain the planet in a stable state. In hindsight, naming the theory after the Greek goddess of the earth was provocative. Moreover, it antagonised the rampant atheists who are apt to attack any idea of faith, mythical or not.

In Gaia, photosynthesising plants produce oxygen as a by-product. However, oxygen is poisonous at high concentrations. So plants release oxygen into the atmosphere as a waste product. As a result, oxygen levels in the atmosphere increased over geological time and created an evolutionary opportunity. An organism that could use oxygen to produce energy would have a massive advantage. The result was the evolution of oxygen-consuming organisms such as animals.

Gaia is a primary feedback mechanism. In this case, the high oxygen availability provides animals with more energy to grow. In return, they release carbon dioxide as a stimulus for plant photosynthesis. Again, a win-win solution supported by evolution.

The Gaia concept implied that the worlds' organisms collaborated to produce homeostasis and a world where life could thrive. Naturally, some Neo-Darwinists and others considered the idea of life cooperating on a world level was preposterous.[110] A few thought Gaia a new-age idea that implied the sacrilege of intent by living organisms. However, in the Gaia model, the apparent purpose arose naturally; it emerged.[111] Also, rather than being flaky, computer scientists expect this result from basic control theory. A complex system with feedback will encourage cooperation and stability, and scientists have known this for decades.[112]

---

[110] Eg: Doolittle W.F. (1981) Is nature really motherly? The Coevolution Quarterly, 58–63.
[111] Holland J.H. (2000) Emergence: From Chaos to Order, Oxford Univ. Press.

Once again, it seems that the idea of nature ruthlessly competing for survival had clouded the establishment's judgement. They knew that evolution worked by competition. Biological cooperation was a myth created by wishful thinking hippies. Lovelock countered Dawkins' almost inevitable objections by creating DaisyWorld.[113] He modelled a planet with two types of plant, black daisies and white daisies. Black daisies absorb sunlight and get hot, warming their surroundings. By contrast, white daisies reflect sunlight back out into space remaining cool. Now the populations adjust and become stable because the growth of the daisies depends on temperature. The result is DaisyWorld maintains a more or less constant temperature despite fluctuations in the incident sunlight.

Richard Dawkins argued that a planet being regulated in this way is impossible without planetary natural selection, whatever that is supposed to mean.[114] He seems to have believed that natural selection was unique and the only way of generating organisation. Dawkins somehow concluded that multiple planets would need to be evolving and competing to create a control system. Such bizarre ideas lacked a reasonable argument or rationality. Presumably, they arose from an almost religious adherence to his particular belief system. He did realise that oxygen and carbon dioxide provides balancing encouragements for exploitation by various organisms. However, this understanding did not extend to appreciating how control systems arise spontaneously.[115]

Updates to DaisyWorld introduced additional species such as rabbits and foxes. Increasing the number of species in this way helped stabilise the planet's temperature. As a result, the system's homeostasis improved, and it recovered quickly back to equilibrium when disturbed. Moreover, perturbing the system helped maintain the species variety. This adaptive response indicates the importance of biodiversity. However, it also illustrates something of fundamental importance; complex systems show adaptive self-organisation and

[112] Ashby W.R. (1956) An Introduction to Cybernetics, Chapman and Hall.
[113] Watson A.J. Lovelock J. (1983) Biological homeostasis of the global environment: the parable of Daisyworld, Tellus B, 35 (4), 286–289.
[114] Dawkins R. (2016) The Extended Phenotype, Oxford Landmark Science.
[115] Ashby W.R. (1960) Design for a Brain, Franklin Classics.

control. One exciting development was the cyberneticist, Ross Ashby, constructing his homeostat machine in the late 1940s.

Following the Second World War, Ashby made use of the available technology. He connected four bomb control units, so they adapted to changing inputs. As the name suggested, the homeostat created its own stabilising controls. When perturbed, the machine would search for a solution and return to its equilibrium. It combed through a set of random conditions until it found one that provided balance. Ashby described such self-organisation as separated parts of a system linking together. He had made a direct demonstration that stability could arise from randomness. He likened the process to learning.

Notably, Ashby's homeostat would generate its own purposeful behaviour. It's what control systems do. As Norbert Wiener explained, "In Ashby's machine, as in Darwin's nature, we have the appearance of a purposefulness in a system which is not purposefully constructed". Wiener suggested that lack of purpose in such systems "is in its very nature transitory".

It is not essential to build in the target. The purpose emerges naturally. As Wiener pointed out, "In an overwhelming majority of cases a machine...will look for purposes which it can fulfil". In other words, machines can develop purpose automatically, and this is expected.

Going further, Ross Ashby would describe an organism's evolutionary adaptation to its environment as returning to equilibrium. Since Ashby's time, self-organisation and order from chaos have become basic ideas in modern science.[116] Self-organisation is a misnomer. As Ashby clearly explained, a basic system does not organise itself. It requires an outside influence or an extra level of control.[117] Physics makes a distinction between open and closed systems. In particular, closed systems obey the second law of thermodynamics. They are observed to become more random and

---

[116] Cybernetics, biocomputing, and chaos theory study such controls arising from recursive feedback loops.
[117] Ashby W.R. (1962) Principles of the self-organizing system, in Principles of Self-Organization: Trans. of the Univ. of Illinois Symposium, H. Von Foerster and G. W. Zopf, Jr. (eds.), Pergamon Press, 255-278.

gradually run down over time. However, open systems can self-organise and communicate with their surroundings.

So not only is self-organisation possible but given suitable conditions, it is expected.[118] Some physicists and computer scientists may consider bizarre the idea that Lovelock would need to generate DaisyWorld to show that Gaia is possible. Since Gaia is merely an elementary control system, which are ubiquitous in manufacturing, robotics, etc. Moreover, such open systems with inherent control are widespread in biology, physics, and chemistry.

## Wallace and Natural Selection as a Control

With remarkable foresight, Alfred Wallace took a systems approach to evolution back in 1858. Wallace described the balance in nature in his initial paper on evolution.[58] He realised that natural selection was a part of something more fundamental–life's control systems.

Other species come in to take the place of an animal with a deficit. "The action of this principle is exactly like that of the centrifugal governor of the steam engine, which checks and corrects any irregularities almost before they become evident". He continued, "in like manner no unbalanced deficiency in the animal kingdom can ever reach any conspicuous magnitude". Wallace believed lack of control "would make itself felt at the very first step, by rendering existence difficult and extinction almost sure soon to follow". Wallace had understood the nature of adaptive control systems and their importance. More than this, he was placing natural selection in context as part of nature's control systems.

Wallace's claim inspired Raj Chakrabarti and colleagues at Princeton. They looked at chains of proteins in the mitochondria that provide energy for the cell. These proteins can act like adaptive machines, possessing the ability to influence their own evolution.[119] The researchers found that the proteins often worked flat out and operated at maximum efficiency, consistent with control theory. It was microevolutionary self-correcting behaviour. The proteins were

---

[118] Prigogine I. (1993) Order Out of Chaos, Flamingo.
[119] Chakrabarti R. (2008) Mutagenic evidence for the optimal control of evolutionary dynamics, Physics Review Letters, 100, 258103.

behaving as if the system was managing itself optimally. They considered they had confirmed Wallace's original proposal about regulation acting like a steam engine's governor.

Chakrabarti suggested their new finding "extends Darwin's model, demonstrating how organisms can subtly direct aspects of their own evolution to create order out of randomness". He continued, "Control theory offers a direct explanation for an otherwise perplexing observation and indicates that evolution is operating according to principles that every engineer knows".[120]

The scientists did not explain how this control came about. Nevertheless, Chakrabarti suggests, "such random processes can create structures capable of steering subsequent evolution toward greater sophistication and complexity". However, he disclaimed the idea that this finding could support intelligent design claims. Unfortunately, such denial appears to be a standard requirement to avoid the wrath of biological atheists.

It is about time scientists stopped apologising for applying basic machine intelligence concepts to cells and organisms. Selfish genes are not the only game in town but a sociopathic dead end. Even a single cell is a massively complex control system with balancing molecular mechanisms. Cells adapt, cells behave, and cells process information.

"What is important is that complex systems, richly cross-connected internally, have complex behaviours, and that these behaviours can be goal-seeking".

William Ross Ashby

---

[120] MacPherson K. (2008) Evolution's new wrinkle: Proteins with cruise control provide new perspective, Princeton Univ. News, Nov 10.

# Mendel and the Modern Synthesis

*"I am convinced that it will not be long before the whole world acknowledges the results of my work".*

Gregor Mendel

As Darwin published The Origin, an Austrian monk Gregor Mendel, the 'father of genetics', conducted his early work on genes. Mendel was a brilliant experimentalist with great scientific taste. He began the new science of genetics by crossing pea plants in a small garden. The peas demonstrated that inheritance could occur in discrete quantities. Genes were objects that separated into dominant and recessive forms and were scattered through the generations.

Mendel's choice of the pea plant was inspired. He had a plant with marked characteristics that were easy to see, such as smooth or wrinkled, green or yellow seeds. He selected peas, crossed the plants, and raised the offspring. Instead of blending to a greeny-yellow colour, crossing a green pea plant with a yellow one gave one green to three yellow offspring. To explain this, he created a theory where discrete genes cause the inheritance, and yellow peas were dominant over the green colour. The parents' genes were randomly shuffled together in the offspring. Mendel's simple experiment laid the foundations for a new science of genetics and an explanation for heredity missing from Darwin's theory.

While Darwin garnered awards and fame, scientists ignored Mendel for decades. It seems that contemporary biologists did not understand the implications of Mendel's experiments. Unlike Darwin, Mendel was not rich and influential. Instead, he took to the cloth to pay for his education and eventually became the Abbot of the monastery. Overloaded with administration in this role, Mendel died lacking recognition in 1884. Then at the start of the new century, scientists rediscovered his experiments. It soon became apparent that combining Mendel's genetics with Darwinian evolution could revolutionise biology.

Paradoxically, the historical narrative suggests Gregor Mendel deserves credit for genetics despite scientists overlooking his ideas for decades. By contrast, we should ignore Patrick Matthew because most biologists were unaware of his discovery for several years. Equally ironically, Darwin deserves recognition for the theory of natural selection as he promoted the concept. When telling such stories, consistency is not required.

The end of the 19th and early 20th centuries witnessed an eclipse of Darwinism.[121] Natural selection was thought to have been overhyped, and some scientists believed it was discredited.[122] One of the problems was that Darwin's ideas led to blending inheritance that was not supported by observation. Moreover, evolutionists telling natural selection just-so stories did not seem to be helping scientific progress. Mendel saved Darwin by providing an inheritance mechanism. Traits would be passed on discretely by genes rather than mixing together in the offspring.

Biologists realised that Mendel overcame one of the main limitations of Darwin's work. Features did not merge. Furthermore, it was easy to follow what happens to the genes when two organisms mate. Thus, a scientist could track a single gene through the generations.

## The Modern Synthesis

The modern synthesis combines Darwin's natural selection and population genetics. In the early 20th century, some scientists realised that adding Mendel's genes to Darwin's natural selection created a more complete theory. Once Mendel's ground rules were in place, the rest was straightforward. Mendel had shown the way, and a reasonably competent scientist would have little difficulty fleshing out the theory and working through the consequences.

Later Crick and Watson determined the double helix structure of DNA. Cells now had a simple molecular way of copying genes. The picture of genes as DNA added to belief in the Neo-Darwinian model where natural selection caused evolutionary change. Then

---

[121] Huxley J. (1942). Evolution: The Modern Synthesis. Allen and Unwin.
[122] Bowler P.J. (1983) The Eclipse of Darwinism, Johns Hopkins Univ. Press.

breaking the genetic code demonstrated the logic of how genes produced proteins. It all fitted with Neo-Darwinian ideas.[123]

Ronald Fisher was one of three leading scientists who took Mendel's results and explained what would happen to genes in a population. The other two were brilliant biologists Sewel Wright and J.B.S. Haldane. Fisher is of interest because of his particular character traits and accusations. Sharon McGrayne's book on the history of Bayes Theorem gives a good account of Ronald Fisher's dominance, bullying, and distortion of statistics in the early 20th century.[124] McGrayne characterised Fisher as an intelligent sociopath, but he died in 1962 and cannot defend himself. Nevertheless, it is reasonable to accept Fisher, an ardent supporter of eugenics,[125] was not a nice man.

It would seem that Fisher understood Darwin's reputation was unassailable, but he didn't like playing second fiddle to Mendel. He considered natural selection and genetics as the two grand theories in biology. Fisher was a world-leading statistician and accused Mendel of scientific fraud on flimsy grounds. The title of Fisher's paper suggests his motivation, "Has Mendel's work been rediscovered?"[126] Perhaps by showing Mendel was a fraud, Fisher's work could rank alongside that of Darwin. Whatever Fisher's motivation, his accusation was bizarre. Imagine crashing your car into a tree on the way to the shops and being told it didn't happen. You were mistaken or a liar because it was an unlikely result — that about sums up Fisher's logic.

According to Fisher, Mendel's results were just too good to be true. But not really. They simply deviated from what Fisher expected. For example, Fisher anticipated one of Mendel's results only 45 times in 10,000 experiments. This probability is not enough to accuse a great scientist of fraud. Besides, Fisher broke his own rule. One of Fisher's rules was that you don't apply statistics to an experiment after the event. In his words, "To call in the statistician after the

---

[123] Modern synthesis and Neo-Darwinism are ill defined terms and are here used interchangeably. Neo-Darwinism is here considered the more restrictive form – a hard synthesis if you will.

[124] McGrayne S.B. (2011) The Theory That Would Not Die, Yale Univ. Press.

[125] Norton B. (1978) A fashionable fallacy defended, New Scientist, 27 April.

[126] Fisher R.A. (1936) Has Mendel's work been rediscovered? Annals of Sci., 1:2, 115-137.

experiment is done may be no more than asking him to perform a post-mortem examination: he may be able to say what the experiment died of".

Fisher's criticism was spurious since there was enough detail for anyone competent to reproduce Mendel's work. The rule is you assume the scientist reported his experiment honestly and correctly, as you can repeat it. In this case, even a class in a school could plant some peas and count the results. Fisher repeating Mendel's experiments would have been easy; he was head of Rothamsted, a world-leading agricultural research centre, for 14 years (from 1919 to 1933). However, Fisher was not disputing Mendel's obviously correct findings. Instead, he was using his position as a top statistician to cast doubt on Mendel's honesty.

Fisher wrongly assumed Mendel had performed his experiment in a specific way. However, Mendel did not describe his research in such meticulous detail. In practice, covering every step might have taken a whole book, like recounting a trip to the shops one step at a time. Moreover, many possible variations of what Mendel did would invalidate Fisher's allegations. For example, gardeners don't expect all seeds to germinate and develop; some seedlings perish. When growing new plants, gardeners often sow several seeds close to each other in a group and select the healthiest looking seedlings. So when Mendel wrote that he planted ten, he might well have buried 30 or more to obtain ten healthy plants.

Mendel had a superb biological understanding and exceptional experimental technique. Finally, we have his brief description of his experiments. He might have supplied more detail, but no one seemed interested in his work. So we don't know the precise details of how he selected, identified, or pollinated his plants — but unfortunately, mud sticks. Whatever vapid arguments Fisher made to sully Mendel's reputation, Mendel was correct, and his findings have stood the test of time.

## Mendel Was Misleading

Sadly, Gregor Mendel's revolutionary results did mislead later biologists. He had given science a way of tracking genes and hints about how they worked. Still, Mendel's results suggested genes explained more than was justified. His single-gene single-effect gave some later biologists the impression of a simple cause and effect relationship — one gene-one trait. For most genes, this was far from reality. Scientists would later find that such Mendelian inheritance is a special case. Most features depend on multiple genes, and there is typically no simple direct cause and effect. Both the environment and development alter gene expression.

Gregor Mendel's genius was to choose a set of unusual genes that caused definite effects in his peas. In effect, Mendel could see the individual genes in the adult plants. He had chosen one of the few plants with a simple relationship between genes and outcomes. For example, single genes change the appearance of the peas, from wrinkled to smooth. While this is unusual, Mendel had inadvertently given the impression that most genes acted in this definite way. The features of animals and plants are not readily associated with single genes, and the effects are not so clear-cut. A different plant or different traits would not have given such concrete results.

Height depends on multiple genes, the environment, and nutrition. Tall people tend to have tall children, and well-fed children grow into taller adults than those deprived of food. Similarly, there is no single gene for athletic prowess, longevity, and disease resistance. Later scientists worked on finding the gene for cancer, homosexuality, IQ, left-handedness, and so on, with a profound lack of success. There is often an inherited component but not one caused by a single gene. Other factors may be at work, such as energy production in mitochondria inherited directly from the mother.

There is more to life than genetic determination. We still have much to learn about what genes do. Despite the widespread hype, the actual contribution of genes to the organism and its development is still not established. For example, we have no accurate genetic blueprint or algorithm for building and operating an eye or a brain; or have not found one yet. Scientists know the basics, the genes needed for an eye, how eyes work, evolved, and the sequence of events in embryonic development. Still, we have little understanding of the most critical aspect: the information flow and control of the process. Junk DNA might be hiding some of the detail.

It appears that what was known as junk DNA may be equally important as Mendel's classic protein-producing genes. However, the protein-coding genes make up only about 2% of our DNA. Scientists called the other 98% junk because they did not know what it was for! Predictably, some Neo-Darwinists suggested it was just selfish DNA hanging around to propagate at our expense.

We now know that some of the so-called junk DNA codes for RNA. RNA is DNA's more dynamic, single-stranded sister that converts DNA code into protein strings. It can also act as a gene controller and is a part of some cell components. Also, RNA may occasionally work as an enzyme and perform some of the other roles of proteins.

When outside observers look at a complex system such as a cell, they perceive arbitrary parts of the whole. In this case, devout Neo-Darwinists might see classical genes and junk DNA. Whereas an epigeneticist appreciates junk DNA as layers of controls. Changing the observer's viewpoint can lead to a different perspective of a dynamic system such as the cell.[117]

## Evo-Devo

The science of evolutionary development, or evo-devo, is hundreds of years old but has recently become fashionable.[127] An old view was that genes coded for something directly, such as smooth peas. So the genome was like a blueprint for the organism. Evo-devo now focuses on a more dynamic understanding of how genes work.

Biologists describe specific control genes as making up the evo-devo toolkit. This toolkit helps regulate the development of the embryo. To take a classic example, developmental biologist Walter Gehring found genes involved in developing the human eye in fruit flies. The genes were the same despite the difference in the structure and function of the two eyes. Then scientists found the genes in squid. Biologists had thought that mammal, insect, and mollusc eyes were entirely different and evolved separately. Still, the same group of genes controlled them all. These toolkit genes were involved in the development of the body plan rather than the tissues.

---

[127] Carroll S.B. (2011) Endless Forms Most Beautiful, Quercus.

The updated explanation is that most DNA is for low-level control. Sections of junk DNA act as switches. Individually they don't do much. However, one switch can turn on other switches. Groups of switches help control development. Think in terms of a telephone network. You can call up a single person from a billion others. Dialling a number activates a series of switches that ultimately links you directly to your sister in Albuquerque.

The principle is the same whether you use a mobile phone or a landline with an old mechanical relay system in a telephone exchange. ON or OFF controls specify a single phone amongst billions. Switches are a way of massively increasing the useful information genes can provide. The switch genes often code for RNA rather than proteins. They cascade instructions and timing down to the protein forming genes.

The human body contains hundreds of different types of specialist cells. Endocrine cells secrete hormones; epithelial cells form the skin and other sheets, and fat cells store energy. Most cells are microscopically small, but some nerve cells extend from the toes to the spinal cord. Despite their varied structure and behaviour, all these human cells contain the same genes. Something else is at work. Since one set of genes produces many different cell types, the genes do not control the cell.[128] Instead, the genes need a controller.

Ultimately, cells and cell signalling trigger the genes.[129,130] For example, in the early stages of development, the embryo releases retinoic acid, similar to vitamin A. It diffuses through the tissue setting up a concentration gradient that tells cells their position. Giving cells their place in the embryo also tells them what to do. It instructs genes in the evo-devo toolkit to begin developmental switching to create an eye or leg. The genes are subroutines in a greater development program.

Whole animals and their activities are even further removed from genetic controls. Of course, this separation does not mean that genes

---

[128] Asserting gene selection in different cells does not overcome the need for control logic.
[129] Mallo M. Alonso C.R. (2013) The regulation of Hox gene expression during animal development, Development, 140: 3951-3963.
[130] Rhinn M. Dollé P. (2012) Retinoic acid signalling during development, Development, 139, 843-858.

do not influence many human characteristics. Still, the available data suggest biologists should be critical of wild claims such as animals are disposable meat machines at the mercy of selfish genes.

As described earlier, a gene classically produced a protein sequence. Still, even the first step in which a protein string folds into a practical shape is not well understood. Proteins are long molecules that can fold like tangled strings. The way they fold is critical to the way they work. There is an astronomical number of possibilities for folding a single small protein molecule. Despite this, new proteins fold fast and often spontaneously to produce stable molecules.

The way proteins fold is critical. For example, mad cow disease, or bovine spongiform encephalopathy, occurs when a short protein called a prion is misfolded. Prion diseases probably include Creutzfeldt-Jakob disease in humans, scrapie in sheep, and chronic wasting disease in deer. In addition, prions may cause many human forms of neurodegenerative disease and dementia, such as Parkinson's or Alzheimer's. The mechanism is telling. If one molecule becomes misfolded, it acts as a template for reshaping others. That is, prions reproduce and spread.

A regular but oddly folded molecule causes infectious prion diseases. Thus, mad cow disease in contaminated meat can spread like a virus despite being merely an oddly shaped small protein. The genetics and nature of the protein are precisely the same as in the healthy form. All that has changed is the way it folded. The misfolding is subject to a form of Darwinian selection. As such, these simple short proteins can evolve and reproduce over time. Prions are an illustration that DNA is not uniquely necessary for natural selection or evolution to occur.[131,132] There are many similar examples of biological change that do not involve genetics.[133]

---

[131] Eg: Uller T. (2013) Non-genetic inheritance and evolution, Philosophy of Biology, 267-287; Toth M. (2015) Mechanisms of non-genetic inheritance and psychiatric disorders, Neuropsychopharmacol, 40, 129–140.
[132] Adrian-Kalchhauser I. *et al* (2020) Understanding 'non-genetic' inheritance: Insights from Molecular-Evolutionary Crosstalk, Trends in Ecology & Evolution, 35(12), 1078-1089.
[133] Eg: English S. *et al* (2015) The information value of non-genetic inheritance in plants and animals, PLoS ONE, 10(1), e0116996.

Part of the issue is that biologists based Neo-Darwinism on large organisms, plants, and animals. Such organisms are relatively rare. There are more ants than elephants and more bacteria than ants. Tiny organisms dominate life, and there are uncountable numbers of microorganisms. But, as we know, bacteria swap and dispense with genes as necessary. Such exchange in the most abundant organisms questions the idea that the gene is the fundamental element in evolution.

In the new way of looking at things, genes code for some of the cells hardware components. They control the development of the protein building blocks. However, these components are part of a greater control system. Assuming genes specify the cell is like saying: since houses are built of bricks, the bricks must be the architect.

Genes specify components, not the cell's control.

The initial idea was that DNA acts as a plan for producing an organism and its behaviour. Nevertheless, there is not enough information. Something else is going on. The length of DNA in humans is about three billion base pairs, and most of this is junk DNA.[134] A cheap and second-rate memory stick could contain all this information with room to spare.

Biologists estimate the total number of human genes that code for proteins to be around 22,000. Which is about the same number of genes as a microscopic worm. Scientists amusingly suggest humans share half their genes with the banana, 60% with the fruit fly, and 85% with mice. How such similar genes contribute to creating these utterly different organisms is not fully established.

## Extended Synthesis

Some biologists realised that the modern synthesis is unnecessarily narrow and have suggested a broadening of evolutionary theory.[135] They recommend extending the focus of natural selection from the gene to groups and populations. The idea is to include epigenetic inheritance, evo-devo, and an organism's ability to be adaptive. The

---

[134] Carey N. (2015) Junk DNA, Icon Books.
[135] Jablonka E. Lamb M.J. (2020) Inheritance systems and the extended synthesis, Elements in the Philosophy of Biology, Cambridge Univ. Press.

extended synthesis acknowledges an organism can alter its environment, which can affect future generations. It also recognises the potential evolutionary effects of self-organisation.

This extended synthesis is not a theory but a collection of factors left out of the modern synthesis. First, there is a return to bodily change occurring before genetic modification. Second, these phenotypic changes are advantageous and occur throughout a population, acting on a group rather than an individual. Finally, the extended synthesis considers factors related to adaptation and fitness. While some of this can cover Lamarckian ground, the explanations are updated.

Jean-Baptiste Lamarck suggested the inheritance of acquired characteristics. The idea is that an organism can pass onto its offspring features that it picked up during its lifetime by use or misuse. If this were correct, bodybuilding might produce muscular children. The idea is wide of the mark, but it is not stupid. Darwin, for example, allowed for use or misuse influencing evolution. We can consider Lamarckism an early and incomplete attempt to build an evolution theory based on fitness.

Notably, the extended synthesis includes the Baldwin Effect and learning. Named after James Baldwin, the effect appears similar to Lamarckian inheritance, but the proposed mechanism is different. For example, when an animal moves to a new environment, it responds by changing its behaviour to match the new conditions. In addition, the animal might teach its new behaviour to its offspring, which affects their reproductive success and future selection.

Surprisingly the Baldwin Effect has even found a place in the modern synthesis. Daniel Dennett suggested that it is when a species pre-tests a particular design. If an organism discovers a winning niche, it will generate a correspondingly reduced selection pressure.[136] The behaviour might come to be encoded in the DNA in some way. Dennett says the Baldwin Effect is just another natural selection application, a crane rather than a skyhook.

---

[136] Dennett D. (2003) The Baldwin Effect: a crane, not a skyhook, in Evolution and Learning: The Baldwin Effect Reconsidered, eds. Weber B.H. Depew D.J., MIT Press.

My objection to the Baldwin Effect is it is ignoring a more parsimonious explanation. The animal decides to move to a new environment and behaves accordingly. It determines its selection pressures by choosing where to live, its neighbours, and the food it eats. The offspring learn from their parents. Baldwin's idea becomes more natural when behaviour is the ultimate driving factor.

The extended synthesis takes us away slightly from the idea that genes explain evolution using natural selection. It acknowledges that there is a lot more going on. One of the drivers for the extended synthesis was the idea of punctuated equilibrium. Evolutionary biologists Niles Eldridge and Stephen Jay Gould noticed that the fossil record was at odds with Darwin's gradualism. Darwin had argued that evolution must be gradual, a slow accumulation of small changes. However, fossils suggest that species are often stable with little apparent change, perhaps for millions of years.

Evolutionary change is often limited to periods of rapid modification and speciation. For some reason, the biological establishment considered this a significant challenge. In reality, whether changes occurred quickly or more slowly would depend on the selection pressures on the species. A well-adapted species would have little selective pressure, perhaps over a long geological period. However, an alteration in the environment would invite an evolutionary response. Thus, whether the evolutionary change is slow and steady or with long stable periods and rapid changes is an outcome rather than an explanation.

## Rock Pocket Mouse

The rock pocket mouse (or Chaetodipus intermedius) is a threatened species in the southwestern United States and Mexico. Birds and other mammals are its main predators. Most mice have light brown fur and well camouflaged against light coloured rock in the desert. However, some dark-furred pocket mice live in areas of darker volcanic lava. This mouse is somewhat unusual in that a single gene determines the coat colour.[137] As expected, the dark gene was prevalent in the lava mice but mostly absent from the desert's light-coated mice.

---

[137] Melanocortin-1-receptor gene, Mc1r.

Biologists consider the pocket mouse to be a model of genetic evolution. Indeed, it would seem to be straightforward and Mendelian. In this view, predation might determine the colour of the mice on different backgrounds.[138] Notably, the genetics are local to this area, as dark mice on other lava flows link to a different gene.[139]

The standard Neo-Darwinian story would be the mice in the area generally had light-coat genes. Still, there is some natural variation with a small number of mice having dark-coat genes. Allowing for random migration and movement, the mice would spread out over the whole area. Predators then take the more visible mice.

Natural selection means the survivors form two populations: dark mice on the lava and light mice in the desert. The predation determines the gene frequencies. Notice how this approach assumes the mice are too dumb to minimise their risk by choosing where to live and avoiding being eaten.

A more straightforward explanation would be that the mice are aware of how visible they are to predators and choose the safer option. Dark mice live on the lava, and light mice prefer the desert. The genetic result would be identical. This account is a more efficient solution for the mice as the population is at a lower risk of predation.

To those who find this behaviour improbable, consider the chameleon. Most of the colour changes are signalling other chameleons. Still, the animal can modify its coat colour to fit its surroundings.[140] Cuttlefish are the chameleons of the sea but are more adept at active camouflage. Indeed, researchers can train cuttlefish to change their patterning for a food reward. They placed cuttlefish in a black or a white tank, and the animal adapted to match the colour. The biologists inserted a black or white signalling probe and gave a food reward if the mollusc broke cover. The cuttlefish

[138] Hoekstra H.E. *et al* (2004) Ecological genetics of adaptive color polymorphism in pocket mice: geographic variation in selected and neutral genes, 58(6), 1329-1341.
[139] Nachman M.W. *et al* (2003) The genetic basis of adaptive melanism in pocket mice, Proc. Natl. Acad. Sci. U S A, 100(9), 5268-5273.
[140] Stuart-Fox D. Moussalli A. (2008) Selection for social signalling drives the evolution of chameleon colour change, PLoS Biol., 6(1), e25.

were able to learn, showing that they had some control of the process. They can be flexible and learn with experience.

The main point here is that assuming that animals are dumb may be confusing evolutionary studies. By not considering animal cognition, scientists avoid simpler explanations. In the pocket mouse case, the natural selection model could be hiding the more parsimonious idea that the mouse makes a decision. For the pocket mice example, there is no data to decide which explanation is correct. However, it would be wise to consider cognition when applying the natural selection narrative. It takes a dumb biologist to think animals are dumb.

"Natural selection eliminates and maybe maintains, but it doesn't create... Neo-Darwinists say that new species emerge when mutations occur and modify an organism. I was taught over and over again that the accumulation of random mutations led to evolutionary change [which] led to new species. I believed it until I looked for evidence".

Lynn Margulis

# Beyond Neo-Darwinism

*"Evolution no doubt occurs, and it's been seen to occur, and it's occurring now. Everyone who's scientific-minded agrees with that. The question is, how does it occur? And that's where everyone parts company".*

Lynn Margulis

Misplaced confidence is a nasty disease from which scientific model builders often suffer. People can confuse the model with reality. For example, some scientists felt internal consistency supported the idea that Neo-Darwinism explains evolutionary biology. All evolutionary biology. They no longer felt the need for testing their ideas by direct observation and experiment. Instead, the theory explains everything by generating narratives. The stories are easy to produce, convincing to some, and meaningless.

Combining Darwin with genetics was particularly subject to this illusion. Mendel provided the rigour of symbol manipulation, which tracked genes with mathematical precision. A brilliant solution. So biologists could dispense with physics envy. To expand the pie to evolution as a whole, it was merely necessary for the Neo-Darwinists to assume that all inheritance occurred through genes. Darwin's theory already claimed that natural selection explained the origin of species and evolution. So now, supposing all inheritance was genetic gave a superficially complete explanation of life. If this were the case, they could turn Darwin's wishy-washy stories into mathematics.[141]

There was still an issue as a single organism contained loads of genes. Moreover, the organism is the target of Darwinian selection. It lives or dies, taking the genes with it. Uncomfortably, genes had no independent existence and were secondary to life. The solution was simple: assume the gene is the primary unit of evolution. So we are to forget about cells and organisms; plants and animals are just

---

[141] The mathematics are quite simple and the stories keep coming.

unnecessary complications. These genetic assumptions made the model so much more straightforward.

Some considered the organism a sort of artefact that the genes needed — the classic throwaway meat robot. Genes were supposedly the only thing consistent through the generations; Richard Dawkins popularised this approach in his unique way. "We are machines built by DNA whose purpose is to make more copies of the same DNA. ... This is exactly what we are for. We are machines for propagating DNA, and the propagation of DNA is a self-sustaining process. It is every living object's sole reason for living". They had taken an excellent model to absurd lengths and lost their way. Remove the wild conjectures, and Neo-Darwinism has value.

## Of Mice and Midwife Toads

August Weismann was a great evolutionary biologist. He realised that the body cells are separate from the sperm and egg cells. Weismann believed that this separation produced a barrier that prevented the inheritance of acquired characteristics, and therefore Lamarck was wrong. Nowadays, we can add to Weismann's objection, as we know that the DNA in the sex cells is even more isolated. The barrier between acquired information and DNA is even stronger than Weismann claimed. There is no direct way for a cell to convert learning into new genes. The genetic code is essentially read-only.[142]

Weismann performed a celebrated but unfortunate experimental test of Lamarckism and found it wanting. In 1887, he started with seven female and five male white mice.[143] He cut off their tails. After recovery and breeding, the mice gave birth to two families the following month. Unsurprisingly, the young offspring had perfectly normal tails. Weismann followed five generations of mice he disfigured in this way. There was no difference between the hundreds of mutilated mice's tails and normal (unmutilated) mice over the generations. Some found the experiment shocking, if not completely

---

[142] A simplification as the enzyme reverse transcriptase generates DNA from RNA.
[143] Weismann (1888), The supposed transmission of mutilations, Lecture at the Meeting of the Association of German Naturalists, Cologne, September.

silly. Playwright and vegetarian George Bernard Shaw reputedly responded: "Seriously Weismann, enough is enough".

Weismann realised that this experiment left a lot to be desired and did not show that mutilations are not inherited. Moreover, it ignored Darwin's gradualism; it might take an impractical number of generations before the inheritance could be observed. However, at least Weismann realised that he should test claims such as inheritance of mutilations by experiment. Still, his investigation was amusingly redundant, as some human groups have practised circumcision for many generations without noticeable inheritance.

It is not clear why Weismann's weak experiment became a standard in refuting Lamarck, whose idea did not involve mutilation but use and misuse. As experiments go, Weismann's mouse trial was rudimentary and inadequate. I included it here in contrast to Paul Kammerer's studies of the midwife toad.

## Midwife Toad

Paul Kammerer was a famous Austrian biologist who considered that evolution could involve acquired inheritance. In short, he was a Lamarckian. Kammerer tried a more realistic experiment than Weismann's to test the possibility of acquired characteristics.[144] Midwife toads are a genus of frog that lives widespread in Europe and North Africa. It is so named because the male acts as a midwife in that it carries and incubates fertilised eggs on its back. When the time arrives, the male enters the water to release the tadpoles.

The toads usually mate on land, but Kammerer managed to convert them to sex in water. He achieved this by increasing the temperature, and the toads entered the water to cool. Over the next two generations, the male toads gained rough, dark nuptial pads on their feet that helped them hold onto the female when mating. Kammerer thought the pads were an acquired characteristic. The frogs were adapting to the new conditions.

All but one of Kammerer's specimen frogs were lost during the First World War. Kammerer had sent the remaining preserved frog to leading biologists in England who examined the specimen. The

---

[144] Hofrichter R. (2000) Amphibians, Firefly Books.

scientist who coined the name genetics, William Bateson, suggested the result was fraudulent but did not provide data. However, in 1926 a direct accusation of fraud was published in the leading journal Nature.[145] Gladwyn Noble, a zoologist at the American Museum of Natural History, claimed that someone had injected the remaining frog's nuptial pads with Indian ink. Thus, somebody, presumably Kammerer, had fabricated the specimen.

Kammerer responded that he re-examined the specimen and confirmed that someone had indeed injected ink. A lab assistant might have done this. Shortly after the ink discovery, Kammerer blew his brains out in the Austrian mountains. He left a note donating his body to science. Other biologists took this act of suicide as an admission of guilt.

Years later, Arthur Koestler, a writer who had been a student in Vienna, examined the original Kammerer papers. He thought he would be writing about a tragic case of scientific fraud. However, Kammerer seemed to be a gentle, caring, and honest individual. The more Koestler delved into the topic, the more bitterness and backbiting he found. People wished to discredit Kammerer because of his support of Lamarck. Koestler found himself unexpectedly supporting Kammerer and thought it likely that he was honest. His critics should repeat the experiment rather than throwing accusations.[146] Replication is at the heart of the scientific method and avoids uninformed and nasty claims of fraud.

As with Mendel, a general rule in science is to assume that a scientist experiments honestly. The researcher may be misguided, incompetent, or downright thick, but you accept he is truthful. In Kammerer's case, the evidence against him was a single specimen that British scientists had long since examined without finding a problem. The toad could have been tampered with some time after being sent to England. It is also possible that a colleague innocently injected the pads to enhance a dark patch that was fading over time. Fading pads might have been misleading. It was, after all, just an illustration and no longer part of an experiment. Then again, a person wishing to discredit Kammerer could have tainted the specimen.

[145] Noble G. (1926) Kammerer's Alytes, Nature, 118(2962), 1476-4687.
[146] Koestler A. (1971) The Case of the Midwife Toad, Hutchinson.

In this case, the presence of Indian ink found years later in the final surviving specimen is not enough to condemn the man or his experiment. The blame was driven more by the fact that Kammerer and his result were Lamarckian and therefore intolerable. Kammerer was actually guilty of getting an unwelcome result. Unlike Weismann, Kammerer's experiment went against the status quo and was thus unacceptable.

At the time, Darwinian evolution could not explain Kammerer's results. However, more recently, epigenetics has uncovered mechanisms by which inheritance can respond directly to environmental change. These findings suggest Kammerer could have been correct and his results reliable. Furthermore, Kammerer's experiment could have switched on some old genes since the Midwife toad's ancestors mated in water and had nuptial pads.

We now know that epigenetics can alter gene expression and that these changes can be inherited.[147] Epigenetics studies change in gene expression. In other words, genes can be switched ON and OFF when adapting to the environment. Notably, Kammerer reported that when he bred the changed toads with normal animals, the traits were inherited in the same way as Mendelian genes. In addition, Kammerer found dominance in the toads' crosses, known as the parent of origin effect. Biologists ignored these epigenetic findings at the time. However, Kammerer's description of parent of origin effects "provides a very specific resemblance, that strongly suggests the authenticity of the midwife toad experiments".[148] Kammerer had given biology an early insight into epigenetics, and an opportunity was lost.

Some biologists are rigidly sticking to the claim that Paul Kammerer was a fraud and his experiment bogus.[149] This claim cost Kammerer his life. They should end this accusation or provide actual

---

[147] Vargas A.O. *et al* (2017) An epigenetic perspective on the midwife toad experiments of Paul Kammerer (1880-1926), J. Exp. Zool. B Mol. Dev. Evol., 328(1-2), 179-192. Vargas A.O. (2009) Did Paul Kammerer discover epigenetic inheritance? J. Exp. Zool. B Mol. Dev. Evol., 312(7), 667-678.
[148] Universidad de Chile (2016) Re-examination suggests Paul Kammerer's scientific 'fraud' was a genuine discovery of epigenetic inheritance, Physics.org, Oct. 31, accessed Jan. 2020.
[149] Gliboff S. (2010) Did Paul Kammerer discover epigenetic inheritance? No and why not, J. Exp. Zool. B Mol. Dev. Evol., 314(8), 616-624.

evidence. A real biologist who does not believe Kammerer would challenge the result by repeating the experiment. Scientists should provisionally accept Kammerer's results short of someone competent doing another trial.[150]

However, Kammerer's findings have little importance to modern biological understanding. If correct, they are merely another example of epigenetics. Taken together with Weismann's mouse-tail experiment, they illustrate profound bias in 20th-century biology.

## Two-Headed Flatworms

We can bring these old-fashioned arguments up to modern times. Planarian flatworms can regenerate. Cut a flatworm in half, and it can repair itself, forming two flatworms. Even a tiny piece of flatworm contains sufficient information to restore the whole organism. "It may almost be called immortal under the edge of the knife".[151] The old assumption was that this is because each cell's DNA has a copy of all the genetic information.

The flatworm's cells appear to cooperate to form an electrochemical map of the complete structure.[152] It is possible to model changes in the electrical map, so the cut parts generate a flatworm with two heads, one at each end. Or form a two-tailed worm without a head. Cut out its middle section and a two-headed flatworm might regenerate both heads. Importantly, there is no gene for the number of heads. Thus, the control system for development is in the organism rather than the genome. This result puts Weismann's cutting the tails off mice into context.

## Darwin and Wallace

Darwin's original problem of evolution was to explain how species change over time. Both Darwin and Wallace were asking where species came from. They started with the idea that the organism was subject to selection. This idea is logical, as it is the organism that lives, dies, and reproduces. Thus, the organism is the

[150] "Someone competent" – as not all scientists are peers!
[151] Dalyell J.G. (1814) Observations on Some Interesting Phenomena in Animal physiology Exhibited by Several Species of Planariae, Archibald Constable.
[152] Pietak A. et al (2019) Neural control of body-plan axis in regenerating planaria, PLOS Computational Biology, https://doi.org/10.1371/journal.pcbi.1006904.

target of evolution. If succeeding generations were different, the changes could accumulate to produce another species over many generations. Thus, natural selection was a way of accounting for new species of *organisms*.

Trying to model organisms is difficult as each is a vast collection of variable genes doing various things. Thus, there was pressure to turn the original evolutionary problem of how species originate into how genes change with time. Why not? It makes things easy to calculate. As the physicist Lord Kelvin put it, "When you can measure what you are speaking about, and express it in numbers, you know something about it". However, this changes the question. We are no longer dealing with the origin of species but following genes.

Evolutionary biologist George Williams was Richard Dawkins inspiration. Both held the view that the gene is the only replicator of evolution. The central dogma of biology is that information only passes from genes to the cell and not the other way around.[153] To some, this suggests that genes must be in control and be the thing that replicates. After all, DNA can hold information accurately, generation after generation.

George Williams repudiated the observed species changes. He argued that "natural selection of phenotypes [actual animals] cannot in itself produce cumulative change, because phenotypes are extremely temporary manifestations". However, this idea is, at best, misleading. Individuals vary, but species consist of organisms of the same structural form that may persist for millions of years. Furthermore, Williams' suggestion is, at best, limited to the large organisms considered by Neo-Darwinism.

To bacteria, genes are throwaway items. If they need more genes, they pick up the necessary plasmid. So it is baffling to promote the primary importance of genes when the most abundant organisms share DNA like human adolescents share computer games.

## Replicators

The survival of DNA requires a functioning cell. DNA is just a chemical. It sits there and does nothing except hold information —

---

[153] DNA makes RNA, and RNA makes protein.

the chemical equivalent of a recipe book for proteins. Notably, gene mutations might improve an organism's survival chances but much more likely will have no effect whatsoever or result in death.

Genes are not replicators. Cells copy DNA with active error checking and correction. Replicating DNA is error-prone, and the cell needs extensive inspection and repair mechanisms. The cell copies, verifies, and corrects errors in DNA. In other words, cells use DNA as memory storage for proteins. Without a functioning cell, DNA is useless.

Generally speaking, genes are a side issue for replication. They are not essential. John von Neumann and others demonstrated that machines and other systems could self-replicate.[154] So at this stage in the book, it should be unnecessary to point out that DNA is a component, and a memory stick is not a computer.

For life, the cell is the real biological replicator. Cells reproduce themselves. The history of life on earth is the lineage of one cell begetting another. As Rudolf Virchow put it in 1858, "All cells come from cells".

Virchow pointed out the three laws of cell theory. One, all living things are composed of one or more cells. Two, the cell is the basic unit of life. And three, cells replicate. Over more than three billion years, cells have been reproducing. Each cell is a copy of its parents. For most of life's existence, life consisted of bacteria or tiny single-celled organisms. Bacteria are practically immortal. A bacterium splits in half to reproduce itself, forming two new cells. In a sense, all bacteria are indistinguishable copies of their ancient ancestors.

Cells come from cells – they replicate.

So it takes a cell to create a cell. At a higher level, a fossil shark may have similar anatomy to a living animal. Both sharks were responding to matching survival pressures. Moreover, while a modern shark may have comparable anatomy and way of life to its ancestor, this does not mean the genes are identical. Many genetic mutations may have been irrelevant. Quite disparate animals can have similar body forms because of convergent evolution. A classic

---

[154] Freitas R.A. Merkle R.C. (2004) Kinematic Self-Replicating Machines, Landes Bioscience.

example is how dolphins (modern mammals) have a similar body form to ichthyosaurs (ancient marine reptiles). The extent to which genes can explain anatomy and behaviour remains to be established.

Dawkins tried to explain his obsession with gene replication using the idea of utility.[155] The term utility has a technical meaning in optimisation and control theory but essentially means usefulness. Utility is not a difficult concept. Philosophers use it as a measure of happiness, pleasure, and ethics. Jeremy Bentham is associated with its origins, as in "the greatest good for the greatest number". Modern ideas about utility taken from cybernetics, engineering, and systems theory are applied in economics and other social sciences. For example, economists might measure the value or use that customers get from a product or service as a utility.

Dawkins was a little confused; he claims "'utility function' is a technical term not of engineers but of economists". For him, it means "that which is maximized". Of course, engineers may like to differ. Fundamentally, utility is a property of systems. In science, utility can be maximised, but it can also be minimised, squared, or averaged, and so on.

Bizarrely, Dawkins suggests that only a gene can have a utility function. "The true utility function of life, that which is being maximized in the natural world, is DNA survival". It is incomprehensible how anyone can misunderstand utility in this way. Utility is just a way of measuring value, convenience, or service. For DNA or any other inanimate chemical, these concepts have no meaning. DNA's utility is to the cell.

Evolutionary utility to a species is something that benefits fitness to reproduce and survive. Survival and reproduction are what really matter. The organism may be a Turing machine capable of all of this with the right program. Notably, the program may be stored in many ways. A demand that the program is written in the genes requires validation. Which genes? Where are the instructions? The onus is on Neo-Darwinists to demonstrate that DNA explains dynamic structure, function, and behaviour. Otherwise, life is a property of the organism.

---

[155] Dawkins R. (1995) River Out of Eden, Basic Books.

111

## An Extended Phenotype?

Perhaps the more egregious and widespread flight of fantasy about genes is Dawkins' extended phenotype. This myth expands the Neo-Darwinian idea that genes control the body and its growth to just about anything the animal creates or does. So genetics explain a beaver's dam, an ant's nest, and a spider's web. Let's take this one absurd step further and claim that genes encoded the works of Isaac Newton, Leonardo da Vinci, and Isambard Kingdom Brunel. Of course, Dawkins realises that genes are only involved in the generation of proteins or RNA. However, he still claims that genes control a bird building its nest without explaining how this is done.

At least Darwin suggested refutations to his theory. He realised it needed to be falsifiable. "If it could be demonstrated that any complex organ existed, which could not possibly have been formed by numerous, successive, slight modifications, my theory would absolutely break down".

Still, Darwin placed the burden on his critics. They have to show there is *no possible way* that natural selection could form, say, an eye over millions of years. Furthermore, should you show that an eye could not develop this way, the response might be: yes, but natural selection creates everything else.

To explain development using genes is an open challenge but imagining that they control behaviour is an even bigger stretch. So we are back at what is required to build an organism such as a robot spider.

A robot web-spinning spider is a demanding engineering undertaking. The construction cannot be pre-packaged but needs to be adaptive. The spider needs to fit the web to the environment's geometry. Each web structure will be different and have its own challenges. The twigs on that bush need to be chosen. The branches will move with the prevailing winds, and our robot spider needs to consider the imposed stresses. Like fishermen, spiders also select sites where they have a good chance of catching their prey. A group of engineers might manage to build a robot spider using advanced methods. Still, it is a problem in adaptive behaviour and control and would probably take years of research and development. Waving hands and saying it's in the genes is not an explanation.

Human brains have utility. A large brain is crucial to human survival, and genes are needed for producing the brains components. The absence of a particular gene can devastate brain function. But something being necessary does not imply it is sufficient. For example, having tyres is essential for a worthwhile motorcycle. However, tyres don't explain how the machine works or is manufactured. They are just necessary components. Similarly, we know genes are needed for proteins, but this tells us little. Perhaps genes are in central control, and cells and animals are merely meat machines. But this has not been shown!

Genes cannot encode a blueprint of the brain, as our DNA doesn't contain enough data. As we have seen, the human genome contains a limited amount of information – a maximum of a few billion bits. Furthermore, people are genetically similar. Two humans are said to differ genetically by only about 0.1%. Notably, scientists do not know how genes might specify and control a brain's billions of cells and trillions of connections. There is not even a plausible mechanism being proposed.

It could be true, with the brain emerging from genetic code by a yet unknown dynamical program working at the edge of chaos. But scientists have little idea of how it might be done. For example, despite years of searching, there is no gene for schizophrenia. If one identical twin has schizophrenia, the other twin has about a 50-50 chance of having the disease. Heredity is more a propensity than a cause.

## Cuckoo Science

Consider the cuckoo, which does not build its own next and inserts its eggs for other species to hatch and parent. Cuckoo chicks get the host birds to provide them with food. Lots of food as they are often much larger than the host bird's young. How they do this is at least partly understood. A description of the cuckoo and its host is all about behaviour.

The interesting question is not can we tell a hand-waving story about how natural selection can produce this activity based on genes.

It is how the brains of the cuckoo and host are dealing with the challenges. The cuckoo and host are in an arms race but for smarts rather than genetic change.

A hungry baby cuckoo colour signals with its large beak and sends out the host's specific feed-me call. The cuckoo chick's feed-me signal is louder, more intense and repeated more often than a host chick's. The strength of these signals induces the host parents to work harder to feed the parasite. The explanation is in terms of communication with the cuckoo influencing the host's behaviour.[156]

We know that the cuckoo is copying and intensifying the feed me signals to the host parents. Cuckoos specialise in parasitizing a specific host variety or species. To do this, they need to recognise their target. Find and keep watch on the nest until it contains eggs and is clear of the parent birds. Then, quickly fly to the nest to lay an egg. If the target species nest is unavailable when the cuckoo is about to lay, it must choose another nest. Lay the egg quickly in the new nest and take away one of the host's eggs. It's an arms race with the host trying to outwit the parasite. So the cuckoo's eggs have to match the target in terms of colour, pattern, and size to fool the parents.

Notably, the cuckoo needs to know its own variety. It has to recognise others of its own subspecies when searching for a mate. Since it has a specific host, it cannot just mate with any available cuckoo. It needs a mate that is compatible with spoofing the particular target species. Since the developing cuckoos have no contact with their parent birds, they inherit this behaviour somehow.

According to Richard Dawkins, evolution has led cuckoos' to manipulate the host birds' nervous system.[114] Dawkins goes even further into a weird flight of fantasy. Rather than dealing with the real cause, biocomputing, Dawkins believes in "genetic action at a distance".

He suggests that the victim's behaviour is to increase the cuckoo genes survival chances. "An animal's behaviour tends to maximize the survival of the genes 'for' that behaviour, whether or not those genes happen to be in the body of the particular animal performing

---

[156] Davies N. (2016) Cuckoo Cheating By Nature, Bloomsbury.

it". This is a strange idea. Ask yourself whether this genetic action at a distance is cause and effect or smoke and mirrors.

Genetic determinism does not fit the available data for development or behaviour. Embryos develop in steps under precise control and depend on communication, timing, and the local environment. It's an information problem. Growth is regulated dynamically in three dimensions, with cells adapting, changing, and moving about. As Alan Turing demonstrated many years ago, these factors may be independent of genes.

## Turing's Blobs

Turing's interest in the brain led to him needing to understand development. As was his way, Turing ignored existing ideas and started again from first principles. In this, he was following the approach of an earlier mathematical biologist Darcy Thompson. Thompson considered natural selection to be an overloaded explanation. Natural selection was present and an influence on evolution but not a sufficient account. Thompson argued that physical and chemical effects influence development, and this directs the possible evolutionary pathways. His classic book, On Growth and Form, provides an alternative narrative.[157]

As might be predicted, Darcy Thomson was criticised for supposedly not understanding evolution and suggesting vitalism. Vitalism is the belief that living organisms have some additional properties to the non-living. In fact, he was mechanistic and discussing physics, engineering, and mathematics.[158] Thompson hinted not at vitalism but at dynamic self-organisation, a topic taken up by Alan Turing and others some years later.

Turing worked with a non-linear approach. This links in with chaos theory, complexity, and systems theory. In particular, he was interested in the emergence of spontaneous order and organisation. Later scientists would follow this line of attack, notably Ilya Prigogine, who received the Nobel Prize for his work. Current

---

[157] Thomson D.W. (1917) On Growth and Form, Cambridge Univ. Press.
[158] Development is an information-dense operation and involves morphogenesis, cell migration, cell suicide, tissue folding, timing, communication, symmetry forming and breaking, epigenetics, dynamic controls, etc.

theoretical biologist, Stuart Kauffman, suggests that emergence provides an alternative explanation for evolution to natural selection.[1] In particular, the cells and tissues might develop through self-organisation rather than being derived from genetics. Importantly, cells are dynamic systems that dissipate energy and reproduce their own complexity.

Even simple dynamic systems are often self-generating and consistent. For example, a whirlpool has an energy-dissipating structure and forms wherever there is an obstruction in a stream. All eddies have a similar spinning geometry and arise naturally. The theory describing water flow hides rules for generating the vortex. Whirlpools form because they are efficient ways of dissipating energy. As the flow speeds up, eddies form on top of eddies resulting in turbulence. Turing realised that with the right conditions, patterns of development in biology could be equally spontaneous.

Turing worked before scientists had found the DNA structure. Nevertheless, he fashioned an explanation for morphogenesis.[160] Morphogenesis is the development of an organism's structure and shape. He demonstrated that a system of chemicals, called morphogens, could spread out and react together, producing patterns. Morphogens create new shapes and include mechanical stress and hormones. For Turing, genes were a type of morphogen.

Turing provided the early stages of an explanation for how complex structures and contrivances form. Nevertheless, Turing's work has not been well understood. It is essentially a computing paper, but as Turing pointed out, understanding it depends on appreciating basic maths, chemistry, engineering, physics, and biology. To aid the reader, Turing provides explanations of the essentials. His clarification shows a compassionate side of Turing that is not typically found in historical accounts.

I met an old Manchester chemistry professor at an award ceremony who had briefly worked on the topic with Turing. Very briefly indeed. We were sitting together as I was receiving

[159] Kauffman S. (2019). A World Beyond Physics. Oxford Univ. Press.
[160] Turing A. (1952) The chemical basis of morphogenesis, Phil. Trans. Roy. Soc., 237 (641), 37–72.

government funds to develop a new form of neural network. The idea of building an electronic brain reminded the old professor about his work with Alan Turing. In the early 1950s, Turing asked the chemistry department for some guidance with chemical reactions. The old professor was a young postgrad student and was assigned to teach Turing a little chemistry. So off goes our young student to Turing's office. He sat down and started describing how chemical reactions work while the great man listened attentively.

"This is all linear. What about non-linear reactions?" asked Turing suddenly and abruptly.

"Oh, we don't do non-linear reactions. It's too difficult. If we find something non-linear, we make a linear approximation to it", replied the student.

"Get out and stop wasting my time!" Turing shouted and sent the confused student back to the chemistry department, where the scientists laughed at the dumb mathematician.

The student, now a professor about to retire, smiled at the memory. Then, he said,

"And guess what? Now, 40-years later, we are just getting into non-linear reactions. I should have listened!"

As usual, Alan Turing had a unique approach to biology. Turing set up a series of equations that change with time. Despite the limitations of 1950s computers, he managed to show that chemical gradients could produce the patterns on a zebra. Of course, Turing worked independently of the chemists and ahead of many of the chaos theorists who would follow.

Turing's was a significant development in how the body might form. He had shown how a leopard might get its spots and a tiger its stripes. It could have lent a hand in bridging the gap between genetic determinism and biological reality. Moreover, Turing was proposing a mechanism explaining how it might happen. The details of Turing's model are not particularly relevant, but he had outlined how organisms could generate complex structures.

Turing's was a more general approach that might explain biological development. The early Manchester computer was slow and limited but enabled him to show the way. The particular two-dimensional chemical patterns that he produced were just an example. He could equally have created the patterns using electric or magnetic fields or vibrations. He expected readers to generalise, just as his Turing machine was not a specific device that used paper tape but a general-purpose computer.

Struggling for the appropriate words, Turing described genes as catalytic. A catalyst is a substance that speeds up or makes possible an otherwise unproductive chemical reaction. He told of an information cascade where a network of chemicals spread out in time and space, forming patterns. In Turing's words, "if a comparison of organisms is not in question, the genes themselves may be eliminated from the discussion". Few biologists realised the implications.

Independently, chemist Boris Belousov famously demonstrated Turing's patterns. Belousov, working in the Soviet Union, had discovered what is now known as the Belousov Zhabotinsky (or BZ) reaction.[161] A mixture of simple chemicals in a dish could produce moving shapes that progressed with wave-like patterns. In other words, a simple mixture was spontaneously generating patterns and information. Belousov struggled to get his results published at the time because other scientists had not understood Turing. They considered Belousov's observations absurd. Patterns and information did not just appear on their own.

They wrongly suggested Belousov's results could not be true as they broke the second law of thermodynamics. While misguided, this rejection was reasonable. As physicist Arthur Edington vividly described, the second law was supreme. "If your theory is found to be against the second law of thermodynamics I give you no hope; there is nothing for it but to collapse in deepest humiliation". But Belousov worked with an open system, and the second law didn't apply. Poor Belousov was trying to get a new discovery that seemed to break the laws of physics published in a scientific journal.

Unfortunately, Belousov was unaware of Turing's work and could not explain his patterns. As a result, scientific journals rejected his

---

[161] Belousov B.P. (1959) A periodic reaction and its mechanism, in collection of short papers on radiation medicine for 1958, Med. Publ., Moscow.

paper, and he could not get it published. This is despite the patterns being an easily repeatable experimental fact. Finally, he managed to publish in a non-peer-reviewed journal in 1959, but it was ignored. A research student Anatol Zhabotinsky was given the task of investigating the reaction sequence and did manage to publish his findings in 1964. The work became well known following a 1968 scientific conference. Unfortunately, new scientific discoveries often meet excessive resistance. In contrast, others are popular for centuries despite having a lack of experimental support.

"We are not the stuff that abides, but patterns that perpetuate themselves".

Norbert Wiener

"The main character of any living system is openness".

Ilya Prigogine

# Simpleminded Games

*"All games share four defining traits: a goal, rules, a feedback system, and voluntary participation".*

*Jane McGonigal*

Perhaps we should begin with an example: the Red Queen hypothesis. The name Red Queen comes from a line in Lewis Carroll's Through the Looking Glass. "Now here you see, it takes all the running you can do, to keep in the same place".[162] Carroll's idea was taken as an analogy to biological competition. The Red Queen and other basic evolutionary games are sometimes presented as breakthroughs in our understanding.[163] However, these stories identify minor feedback loops that are abundant in biology and engineering.

If rabbits evolve to run faster, foxes will go hungry. So evolutionary pressure means faster foxes have a survival advantage as they can still catch the quick rabbits. It's an arms race. Both the predator and prey are locked in a competition of improvement. With no change in behaviour, they both need to keep running faster to stay in the same place (not go extinct). In reality, predators and prey have multiple controls on their populations, which can vary chaotically. For all its appeal, the Red Queen is a simplistic game that needs to be seen in a broader context.

## Games for the Ruthless

The modern Neo-Darwinism narrative depends on game theory. Neo-Darwinism has been perhaps the most natural application of the theory of games. Once again, the improvement was to make the Neo-Darwinian approach seem more rigorous. John von Neumann and Oskar Morgenstern introduced game theory in the 1940s.[164] It

---

[162] Carroll L. (1865) Through the Looking-Glass, Macmillan.
[163] Ridley M. (1994) The Red Queen: Sex and the Evolution of Human Nature, Penguin.
[164] von Neumann J. Morgenstern O. (1980) Theory of Games and Economic Behavior, Princeton Univ. Press.

found immediate application in economics and particularly defence strategy. Perhaps the most well-known use was Mutually Assured Destruction (MAD), where the United States faced the Soviet Union in nuclear escalation. The result was an arms race similar to the Red Queen example. The game of Chicken underpinned it.

Chicken is two car drivers accelerating towards a cliff edge. Neither wants to chicken out and be the first to apply the brakes. Clearly, a good outcome requires one player to chicken out. Sadly, in the cold war and notably the Cuban Missile Crisis, the world's future depended on politicians and military strategists who thought this level of absurdity was appropriate.

By the 1960s Richard Lewontin and others introduced game theory into evolution.[165] He suggested that game theory would solve some issues not covered by genetics and natural selection. Later, John Maynard-Smith and George Price further developed a Neo-Darwinian game theory in the following decade. It seemed a perfect fit, as both were based on cold-blooded competition.

## Games Require Thought

In this book, I have had to get around philosophical arguments against purpose and anthropomorphism. Fortunately, the introduction of game theory into biology makes these arbitrary restrictions absurd. Game theory is the study of the interaction between rational decision-makers. In other words, players have a form of cognition and an aim – to win.

Games require decision-making.

However, evolutionists ignore the implications and the need for organisms to make decisions. Additionally, the elementary game theory they employed has an inbuilt bias. The classic example called the Prisoner's Dilemma shows this prejudice. Ruthless self-interest was a given in this simple game.

Sam and Ned are innocent friends, arrested and kept in separate cells, unable to communicate. The police don't have enough evidence to get a conviction on the main charge. However, they could convict

---

[165] Lewontin R.C. (1961) Evolution and the Theory of Games, J. Theor. Biol., 1(3), 382-403.

on a lesser charge. So the prisoners can betray each other or cooperate and stay silent.

- If both remain silent, both of them will get a year in prison on a lesser charge.
- If Sam and Ned both betray the other, they will both serve two years in prison.
- Say, Sam betrays Ned, who stays silent. Then Sam will be free, but Ned will serve five years, and vice versa.

Prisoner's Dilemma originated in the Rand Corporation think-tank in the 1950s. Rand was created shortly after World War II to concentrate on defence-related issues, particularly operations research. This background gives insight into the bias that clouded their judgement. In Prisoner's Dilemma, Rand created a psychopathic game.[166] Prisoner's Dilemma is a game where a player is encouraged to rat. There are plenty of other less biased games, but Prisoner's Dilemma was promoted.

Rand's solution was to save yourself and drop your friend in it. If Sam ratted on Ned, Sam would go free or serve only two years (if Ned was also a rat). However, if Sam remained silent, he might end up in the slammer for five years. So Rand's rational response is for Sam to drop Ned in it. It is pure self-interest.

Nonetheless, the correct thing to do depends on the precise conditions. A prisoner has to decide on the risk the other will cooperate or defect. If the other prisoner were your loving mother or grandfather, they would likely be trusted to cooperate. By contrast, if the other prisoner was a deranged axe murderer with a grudge against you, it might be wise to assume he will defect.

Your response should depend on your assessment of your friend. How clever is he? Is he intelligent enough to realise that you can both get off with a lesser charge? Do you trust him, and importantly, will he trust you? The risk changes with the narrative. Once again, it depends on the information you have and the story that is applied. Even the words used to describe the game are critical.

---

[166] As Mandy Rice Davies might have put it: well they would, wouldn't they.

The options in the game were specified as cooperate or defect. This choice of words is misleading. If you cooperate with someone, you work with him to achieve something. In this case, the hope is the outcome will result in mutual benefit. However, your collaborating is beneficial to the other but could be costly to you. That is the definition of altruism – helping another at a cost to yourself. However, biologists usually ignore the altruistic element of risky cooperating. Whatever you decide, you will also be cooperating or defecting with the police.

Prisoner's Dilemma is a sociopath's dream game, as the payoff was adjusted so that your rational solution is pure self-interest. It assumes you can trust the police. If you are ever in a situation like that – it is naive to trust your jailer. The police are already regulating the information flow to your detriment, as you cannot communicate with your friend. Such communication could completely change the outcome.

### Evolutionary theorists use sociopathic games.

One problem with this so-called rational approach is real people often behave irrationally. For example, when tested, people often decide to take the risk of acting altruistically. Perhaps, they do not want to be a traitor to their friend or consider a guilty conscience too high a price. This is particularly confusing to sociopaths who have difficultly understanding altruism and are confused when people or animals don't act selfishly.

As game theory moved across into biology its inbuilt sociopathy supported evolutionary ideas. It generated what might be called the selfish gene approach. Richard Dawkins stated it clearly. "So long as DNA is passed on, it does not matter who or what gets hurt in the process. Genes don't care about suffering, because they don't care about anything".[167]

### Assuming ruthless self-interest was a blunder.

Genes were supposed to compete in ways modelled by these simplistic one-off games. Selfish genes associated with the rational outcome will survive while others will go extinct. However, there is a

---

[167] Dawkins R. (1995) God's utility function, Scientific American, Nov, 80-85.

fault in this logic. Evolution is not one game but multiple repeated games occurring over aeons, generation after generation.

## The First Law

To play a game, the player needs a minimum amount of information. It needs to be able to take several states equal to the number of options. A single organism can achieve this with its behaviour. For example, animal brains can make quick decisions. However, a population is necessary for a gene to have multiple states. As a result, Neo-Darwinian selection is slow – very slow. It acts on variations in the gene pool, producing a gradual response over generations if not many millennia.

For natural selection to operate, the organisms must vary. Otherwise, the parent population would contain identical individuals, and selection would be futile. This observation takes us to Ashby's Law, which is sometimes described as the first law of cybernetics.[168] Like natural selection, Ashby's Law is easy to understand and apparently obvious but subtle and profound.

Ross Ashby was an English psychiatrist who, like Alan Turing, was interested in how brains work. While other psychiatrists focused on Freud or Jung's ideas, Ashby realised that understanding the brain would more likely come from Turing's machines. He produced two classic books, Design for a Brain and Introduction to Cybernetics.[115,112] Largely overlooked now and sometimes forgotten, Ashby's work is fundamental to understanding how systems function. Which systems? All systems, including those in biology.

Ashby's Law says if you don't have enough information, you can't solve the problem. Unfortunately, the law is often worded somewhat obscurely, such as "variety absorbs variety". Here the terms variety and information are interchangeable, as the two ideas are inseparable. Perhaps Norbert Wiener put it more clearly when he said, "To live effectively is to live with adequate information".

Variety is the number of different states a system can have. Consider a burglar faced with opening a safe. Here the requisite

---

[168] Ashby's First Law is equivalent to the 10th information theorem, Shannon and Weaver (1948) Mathematical Theory of Communication, Univ. of Illinois.

variety in the safe is the combination. To open the safe, a safecracker might need to dial a combination of three numbers. Unless he is very lucky, he needs to know all three numbers in sequence to open it on the first try. If he knows only two of the three numbers, say 23 and 42, he may need to try all possible values for the third number. It will typically take him a bit longer and require more attempts. To open the safe, the burglar needs to match the complete combination. If the burglar knows the sequence, his variety destroys the variety in the combination lock.

For a biological example, you are lost in the forest and see a cute furry animal. Do you run away or catch it for your supper? The answer might depend on knowing if it is a rabbit or a tiger. It may seem obvious, but you need to know about these animals and their behaviour. You need to be able to see and identify them. Can the tiger see you? Can you run faster than a tiger? What weapons do you have? It's decision time, a quick, life or death decision.

Natural selection is not a straightforward replacement for learning and communication. However, given enough time, it may have the necessary variety to generate a response. Firstly, the population's variety needs to be sufficient to cover the environmental conditions. For example, any population without animals that resist starvation, dehydration, water, cold, and heat would not deal with changing weather. Natural selection does not add information. Indeed, with each generation, the selection removes some variety. Over time, more variety needs to be added to cover that which natural selection removes. In genetics, this is usually explained by random gene mutations or sex. Each random genetic mutation or recombination adds to the variety.

Charles Darwin was working without knowledge of DNA and genetics but realised the problem of the lost variety. Darwin's principle of divergence suggested that a varied population can fit more niches in an environment.[169] They will thus spread out and multiply in varying surroundings. This is Ashby's Law again. Increasing the variety in a population enables it to match more environmental situations and habitats.

---

[169] Uchii S. (2004) Darwin's principle of divergence, presented at the 5th Quadrennial International Fellows Conference, May 26-30.

## Modern Game Theory

Fortunately, the advent of cheap computing fundamentally changed game theory. As it turned out, self-interest was far less helpful than it had appeared to be. By the early 1980s, scientists realised that pure self-interest was a terrible strategy for repeated games. Moreover, it was quickly found that a selfish player was at a severe disadvantage when games were recurring.

Political scientist Robert Axelrod organised a couple of tournaments to find the best strategies for the Prisoner's Dilemma.[170] The idea was a competition to see who could develop the most powerful software solution. Instead of a single game, they would repeat play for 200 moves making the contest nearer to life. Computer engineers, social scientists, and others developed programs they thought might win. Some were simple, while others were considerably more complicated.

In the end, the winner was a simple contestant. Tit-for-tat was victorious in both tournaments, which was a surprise for nearly everyone involved. Tit-for-tat cooperated on the first move and then repeated its opponent's last move. So it started nice and then cooperated if its opponent cooperated, but defected if its opponent defected. Tit-for-tat was a solution that took only a few lines of code. It turned out that advanced programs using sophisticated analysis performed no better than simple strategies.

While Tit-for-tat is not a perfect solution to the Prisoner's Dilemma, it is a straightforward strategy that plays excellently. Also, it is a nice solution, in that it starts by cooperating and just responds to punish defection. Thus, Tit-for-tat was basically cooperative, and this contributed to its success.

Notably, Tit-for-tat's friendly moves were not cooperative in the usual meaning. More accurately, it was altruism potentially benefiting the other player at its own expense. Being nice in this way means a defecting player will reduce Tit-for-tat's score. Despite this, generally cooperative players like Tit-for-tat were superior.

Repeated games showed the dominance of cooperation.

---

[170] Axelrod R. (1980) Effective choice in the Prisoner's Dilemma, J. Con. Res., 24(1), 3-25.

Nice solutions generally did better than nasty ones if they were not too friendly and willing to retaliate. They would often lose a little playing with defectors but would match their opponents result – close to a low-score draw. However, when dealing with other cooperators, both would score high. The high scores with nice players could more than compensate for the losses defectors would inflict. In the tournaments, nasty programs such as Always-defect did not score well.

William Hamilton, the scientist who coined the phrase "selfish gene" and did much of the original research that Richard Dawkins popularised, realised that evolution could depend on cooperation.[171] Axelrod and Hamilton started to consider cooperation in biology. Evolutionary biologists were overlooking many quite evident examples. For example, trees and ants cooperate; trees house and feed the ants, while the ants protect the trees.

Axelrod and Hamilton claimed that biologists ignored cooperative behaviour before the mid 20th century and did not think it needed special attention. My interpretation is somewhat different. Bias in Neo-Darwinism asserted that evolution worked on the survival of the fittest and competition. Thus, it had mistakenly denigrated altruism, cooperation, and teamwork.

## A Dynamic Strategy

John Nash was made famous by the Hollywood film A Beautiful Mind. Nash was interested in strategy and cooperation. The film attempts to explain his most famous result, the Nash Equilibrium.[172] Nash is out drinking with three friends. A blonde and three brunettes walk in, leading Nash and friends to discuss who will get a date with the blonde. John Nash has a revelation – cooperate. "If we all go for the blonde, we block each other, and not a single one of us is going to get her. So then we go for her friends, but they will all give us the cold shoulder because nobody likes to be second choice. But what if no one goes to the blonde? We don't get in each other's way, and we don't insult the other girls. That's the only way we win".

---

[171] Axelrod R. Hamilton W.D. (1981) The evolution of cooperation, Science, 211(4489), 1390-1396.
[172] Webb J.N. (2007) Game Theory: Decisions, Interaction and Evolution, Springer.

Nash worked on the interaction of several players in a game. Let Bob, Dick, Harry, and Alice be the players. The outcome for Alice depends on what the other players decide to do. In the same way, Bob's decision also hinges on what he thinks the others will do. Poor Alice needs to work out what Bob will decide, given what he thinks the others will choose to do. Likewise, Alice's problem applies to Dick and Harry as well. A good decision depends on what everyone thinks everyone else thinks. There is a lot of information processing and modelling going on here.

A Nash Equilibrium is tough to describe well, never mind compute. The solution depends on having an idea of the other players' strategies. Alice needs to be smart enough to figure out what the others are likely to do. She needs to realise that Bob and each of the other players also have a brain. In other words, Alice needs a theory-of-mind for the others. The situation becomes an equilibrium when every player achieves maximum benefit, and no one can gain more by changing strategy.

Nash came up with his idea on equilibria while a student of game theory in 1950.[173] Over the next 40 years, his work had a considerable influence on technology and society. The applications are numerous, including military strategy, transport, and natural resources management. It is beneficial in areas where people with different preferences cooperate. However, its particular use was in economics and finance, such as auctions and preventing bank runs.

John Nash gained the 1994 Nobel Memorial Prize in Economics for his "pioneering analysis of equilibria in the theory of non-cooperative games". Here we are concerned with Nash's approach rather than the idea of stability and equilibrium. Equilibria are static, and life is a dynamic system. The interesting part is his use of theory-of-mind, where Alice recognises Bob as smart.

More recently, similar approaches have developed where Alice thinks she is more sophisticated than the others. This improvement makes the result easier to calculate and can give more valid results than the classic Nash equilibrium.[174] For example, it varies the

[173]Nash J.F. (1950) Non-Cooperative Games, PhD thesis Princeton Univ.
[174] Clippel G. *et al* (2019) Level- k mechanism design, Rev. Econ. Studies, 86(3), 1207–1227.

number of times the cycle goes round and round, where Alice thinks that Bob thinks that Alice thinks… Once again, the main advantage comes from realising the other players can be smart.

## A Stable Strategy?

Geneticist John Maynard Smith was interested in applying something similar to Nash's equilibrium to evolutionary games. He avoided the need for smart organisms by converting John Nash's equilibrium into a degenerate stable strategy. Cognition was removed and replaced by genes and natural selection. Once again, this assumes that organisms are rational, purely self-interested, and at the same time dumb.

Maynard Smith assumed that strategy is inherited and in some way encoded in the genes. So he worked with fixed behaviour and learning over a long evolutionary period. This is reasonable if one accepts both dumb animals and Darwin's idea of gradualism. In other words, Maynard Smith assumes that the players have no awareness or decision-making freedom.

While a Nash equilibrium involves decision-making individuals, Maynard Smith didn't think this appropriate in biology, as only humans are intelligent. Assuming behaviour is limited was also a helpful simplification for building his model. So he modified an organism's strategy by gene mutation and selection. Maynard Smith created an evolutionary stable strategy (ESS) by placing these restrictions on life's games.

Maynard Smith's ESS behaviour is stable in that a competitor's strategy cannot replace it in a population. Moreover, it applies to players with fixed strategies. So, Smith's idea is, at best, a highly degenerate form of Nash Equilibrium.

It is not clear how Smith and others thought the strategy was implemented. Genetically determined or not, it would still need each player to have processing logic and an algorithm. Moreover, the idea that a mutation improves this system is about as sensible as a programmer trying to update your mobile phone by bashing it with a turnip. So we are back with strategies changing over geological time scales. By contrast, learning and cognition are more rapid and efficient processes.

Evolution is a dynamic process,[175] which rewards efficient solutions. An organism is under repeated and rapidly changing challenges. As a result, species have a survival pressure to develop the ability to react quickly and adapt. The agile and resourceful have an advantage. Individuals capable of an immediate decision may be more likely to survive than dumb creatures that require a hundred generations of genetic change for the same choice.

*The evolutionary stable strategy is dumb biology.*

Moreover, Maynard Smith proposed a system for equilibrium, which does not work well in a dynamic evolving system. Since equilibrium is a fixed point or a steady-state that does not change with time. But evolution is change. Consider the contradiction, an EES organism can't be supplanted by another strategy – but evolution involves its replacement.

There were some questionable attempts to extend evolutionary game theory to people. In particular, sociobiology and evolutionary psychology take this approach. These aim to explain social behaviour, including human society, in terms of evolution.[176] Essentially, sociobiology is a form of evolutionary theory applied to society. Firstly, sociobiology assumes some behaviours are inherited. The inherited traits are a result of natural selection acting on genes. Then sociobiology uses ESS to help generate new behavioural ideas.

It may be the case that some human and animal behaviour is biologically determined. However, no behavioural trait is 100% inherited. If there is a heritable component, it typically involves multiple genes, each having a small effect. Single gene links account for up to about one per cent of the variety in a particular behaviour. Moreover, many of the genetic links are currently too small to be measured accurately. Psychologists sometimes describe the problem as missing heritability.

At this point, it should be unnecessary to state that humans and other organisms are not dumb creatures and do not fit the criteria for ESS or sociobiology. By contrast, John Nash's approach is valuable in multiple human applications because it assumes intelligent players.

---

[175] Nowak M.A. (2006) Evolutionary Dynamics: Exploring the Equations of Life, Harvard.
[176] Wilson E.O. (1978) On Human Nature, Harvard.

A more scientific approach to behavioural evolution might be based on Nash and intelligent organisms. You can't explain behaviour by supposing that it is genetically determined in dumb organisms lacking awareness and learning ability.

## Cooperative Games

Neo-Darwinists had introduced a limited form of noncooperative games into biology. They ignored the ubiquitous nature of communication and cooperation; even bacterial colonies and films like tooth plaque collaborate. Notably, some cooperative groups of single-celled organisms provide an evolutionary bridge to the large multicellular creatures. Animals, plants, and fungi generally consist of billions or trillions of cooperating cells. A forest is not just a mishmash of individual plants and animals dominated by trees. It is an ecosystem of competing, collaborating, and communicating organisms.

Look about and what you see is a world of cooperation and symbiosis hidden in full view. Physiologists describe a person in terms of the billions of organised human cells that form the body. However, these cells are numerically small compared with the bacterial cells covering the skin's surface and much of the gut's content. Remove the microorganisms, and the person will sicken and potentially die. The gut bacteria break down our food and provide nutrients in return for nourishment and a home. This is more obvious in the case of the cow. Cows cannot break down cellulose in grass. Instead, they rely on gut bacteria to convert the vegetation to nutrients. Similarly, termites need bacteria to break down wood. Everywhere a naturalist looks, he sees cooperation.

Cooperative games describe how cells, organisms, and species work together. Yet, these cooperative games are the ignored part of evolutionary game theory. Despite the name, they do not start from the idea that the players must cooperate. Instead, there is an outside party to enforce the agreement.

Neo-Darwinian games assume organisms are only able to make self-enforcing contracts. In other words, self-interest is implicit. Organisms can only cooperate if there is something in it for them.

This blind alley is why we find Neo-Darwinists denying altruism or explaining it away as selfishness — altruism without altruism.[67]

By contrast, in cooperative games, cells form groups that can make enforceable contracts. For example, human cells can agree to limit growth and reproduction to form a tissue in the kidney. This agreement is a denial of the cells survival instinct – to grow and reproduce. Instead, they are cooperating with the needs of the body.

The 'contract' is that the cell will behave like a kidney cell. In return, it gets energy and a warm, supportive environment. Notably, the body enforces the contract and issues instructions. Apoptosis is an extreme example when the body issues an instruction telling a cell to commit suicide for the greater good. The body may kill a cell that fails to comply; apoptosis is the gangster's offer the cell can't refuse.

Life's cooperation is everywhere.

In principle, it may be possible to build kidney cell cooperation using reductionist selfish games from the bottom up. However, a top-down approach helps understand such control systems, which may not be evident to those limited by the old selfish view.

Computing provides a familiar example. It is possible to write all software in machine-level code using the binary data and instructions directly. This low-level approach has some advantages. The programmer knows what is happening at the machine logic level and can follow the process in detail. However, programming like this is slow, error-prone, and challenging. Fortunately, software engineers can use machine code to write a higher-level language, such as Basic. High-level languages are easier to use and update. Programmers using high-level languages make fewer mistakes, and the machine becomes more user friendly. The machine code is still there, but the programmer can ignore it.

Often, someone has an idea of simplifying the programming process further and suggests an even higher-level language. One example of this is object-oriented software that represents real-world items. For instance, a genetic algorithm might have cell-objects holding chromosome-objects containing gene-objects. Ultimately, people with little knowledge of computing benefit from the increased simplicity of ever higher-level languages leading to the visual touch screen operating systems and voice controls in modern devices. This means that even people with little to no understanding of how the machines work can use smartphones.

## Ashby's Good Regulator

While evolutionary theorists were locked into their self-reinforcing justification of self-interest, they missed more than life's ubiquitous cooperation. The core element of natural selection is fitness. Fitness is how well an organism can adapt to its environment.

In the language of cybernetics, fitness controls the environment. An adapting organism can compensate for applied environmental stress. Ross Ashby followed up his idea of requisite variety: the minimum information needed to play games effectively. Working with Roger Conant, he came up with the good regulator theorem. A regulator is anything that controls another system, plays a faultless game, or survives in an environment. We can state the theorem as:

Every good regulator of a system must be a model of that system.

An engineer building a control system or a computer scientist writing AI software will immediately recognise the meaning.

Once again, Norbert Wiener put it well, "The best material model of a cat is another, or preferably the same, cat". Unlike biologists, engineers work typically with bad systems, basically, one that is broken or malfunctioning. In creating a control system, the engineer must account for every possible state of the system. Miss one, and the system will fail. Therefore, controls need to cover the whole system: every conceivable event.

Computer scientists are in awe of organisms dealing with the real world's complexity for billions of years. An organism deals with numerous things that behave in unpredictable ways. By contrast, current AI systems work well in limited and well-structured environments. The difficulty with making self-driving cars illustrates the complexity of the real world. Software engineers input the rules of the road and what to do in a world of traffic, pedestrians, and cyclists. But what if that unexpected unicyclist is not covered. The machine can see half a bicycle and thinks the car will hit the bicycle's front wheel. So it brakes hard and veers off the road, oops. Telling the relatives that meeting a unicyclist on the road was a million to one chance may be less than soothing.

In biological terms, a good regulator is a fit organism likely to survive and leave offspring. Conversely, a bad regulator has behaviour that makes it more likely to be eliminated. A system is not good or bad in an absolute sense. We say it's good when it responds effectively to the current challenges. Still, it might become bad when the situation changes. Fitness is dynamic and varies with the circumstances. Fitness is relative.

A good regulator acts to survive and reproduce.

Evolution by natural selection describes a population of animals changing from bad to good regulators over time. That is, unfit animals become fit for their environment.

## Alice Plays Chess

Let's apply the good regulator theorem to games so we can uncover a deeper biological meaning. A story about Alice playing chess will make things clear. When Alice first learns chess, she needs to do a lot of working out for each move. She scans the board carefully, looking a move or two ahead, trying to estimate which is best. The effort is intellectually demanding, and intelligent beginners like Alice have an advantage. Alice is smart, but even so, her early chess playing is pretty bad. She struggles to decide on the best move or look ahead. Learning chess gives Alice a headache.

As Alice advances a little, she learns that there are standard chess openings. An opening is a series of moves that chess experts found is a good strategy for starting a game. When Alice uses an established opening, she does not think much about her moves until her opponent strays from her expectations. As a result, her first five or so moves in most games become almost automatic, requiring only memory. More than that, Alice no longer has to begin by searching the board and trying to look several moves ahead.

What Alice was doing in learning chess openings was increasing her internal variety. She would check the start of play against her known chess openings. Alice could automatically choose the next move if the board was in one of her known opening states. She did

135

not have to analyse the position in depth — her moves were those of chess experts honed over decades.

Following up on openings, Alice discovers there are end game strategies. Towards the end of the game, the players have removed most of the pieces. The massive complexity of possible move sequences has collapsed to something manageable. Alice finds that learning some basic end game theory also helps her play.

Alice improves her play and starts entering chess competitions. Here she quickly realises that the more successful players have studied many chess openings. Indeed the first half of a match could be just following an accepted sequence. The successful players generally had greater variety and stored more openings in memory. As expected, the more chess theory Alice learned, the more successful she became. Now a strange thing starts happening. Alice no longer struggles to look several moves ahead. She scans the board and checks ahead occasionally but starts to see the board in terms of patterns of play. Alice now feels or sees the best few candidate moves and ignores the rest. She is matching the board to her internal patterns.

Then Alice was introduced to the classic games by grandmasters. Competitors study model games by great players. Books contain annotated games where experts have analysed the winning and losing moves. Following these games gave Alice an increased level of understanding and strategy. Alice persevered, and her game slowly improved. Playing games still required intense concentration but was somehow easier. Things were falling into place.

Alice then had the opportunity to play a leading grandmaster in the national chess competition. The game was an exhibition with the great man, and Alice was chosen as the most suitable opponent. But, of course, she was not expected to win and had little real chance.

Fortunately, Alice realises chess books contain all the important games played by the grandmaster. So, for the six months before the competition, Alice studied the grandmaster's games. The opening he used most often. His approach to attack and how he defends. Gradually she began to get a feel for the grandmaster. She felt as if she knew him and could almost recall all the moves in his hundreds of games. Then she went over the expert commentaries on the games

— the great moves, and more importantly, the poor moves that led to draws or losses. By the time of the exhibition, Alice was ready.

The game itself was not a classic. Alice started with an opening where the grandmaster had struggled in some of his games. She played the middle game carefully until the grandmaster seemed to lose concentration, and Alice pounced. He lost concentration, as it wasn't an important game for him. He made a mistake but might have recovered. However, Alice fought tenaciously, carefully nurturing her slight advantage until the endgame. Both Alice and the grandmaster could see her endgame advantage. He laughed and said, "Great game", while holding out his hand to the winner.

Alice won but not because she was the better player. Instead, she had built a model of his play in her head. In other words, Alice had become what Conant and Ashby described as a good regulator. She knew his game, his strategies, and his errors. Thus, Alice had an internal model of the grandmaster. On this occasion, he played as Alice expected and she won.

In contrast to current computer systems, people can drive cars and do numerous other complex real-world activities. Human brains have a massive internal model of the world. They evolved to survive in a rapidly changing and information-rich environment. Similarly, a monkey is adept at swinging through tree branches. A great black-backed gull superbly selects updrafts while gliding about a cliff face and searching the sea for fish. Below, a herring manoeuvres in a shoal through weeds and rocks at the cliff bottom. Looking up at the gull, the fish takes care she does not become the bird's dinner. To survive, every species must be a good regulator of its environment.

"A brain can improve till it fits its environment".

William Ross Ashby

# Modern Game Theory

*"Shall we play a game?"*

Joshua (WarGames)

An organism's continued survival depends on its decision-making ability, whether the organism is an animal, plant, fungus, or even a microorganism. In a single game, there is no penalty for being mean. The defecting organism gets away with it, as the victim does not have an opportunity to respond. In a repeated game, a victim with memory can hit back on the next cycle. This retaliation is how Tit-for-tat was so successful. While it plays nice with cooperators, Tit-for-tat drives a repeating defector into a backbiting loop of its own making, spiralling down losing points all the way.

## Theory of Mind

William Press and Freeman Dyson demonstrated that a sufficiently intelligent organism with a theory-of-mind could control other players.[177] They identified two types of players, evolutionary and those with a theory-of-mind.

As the name suggests, evolutionary players fit the Neo-Darwinian model. The evolutionary player uses a fixed or simple strategy – Tit-for-tat is an example. Players like Tit-for-tat concentrate on their own reward and ignore their opponent's strategy.

A player with a theory-of-mind understands the opponent. If a player has an internal model of the opponent, they recognise the others strategy and payoff. Press and Dyson describe a player with a theory-of-mind as being "sentient", indicating a higher level of intelligence. For example, they describe Extort a player with a theory-of-mind and show it is a winning strategy.

---

[177] Press W.H. Dyson F.J. (2012) Iterated Prisoner's Dilemma strategies, Proc. Nat. Acad. Sci., 109 (26), 10409-10413.

## Understanding Other Players

Prisoner's Dilemma is a classic game but far removed from the pressures on organisms to survive. As games go, it is not even particularly interesting. One of the issues is that modelling or communicating with the other prisoner is excluded. So let's take a more compelling game.

Bob phones Alice for a date, and they agree to meet. Bob suggests they meet on Saturday in Paris, but Alice's phone catches fire in mid-sentence. Bob and Alice now have no means of communication. What should Alice and Bob do?

After the initial shock, Alice begins to think. She knows Bob is bright, and they both will be thinking about a solution. So Alice meets Bob in Paris on Saturday. But how?

Bob and Alice each have a theory-of-mind, and this changes everything. Alice had an idea that being unable to communicate, Bob would pick the most accessible location. The Eifel Tower is perhaps the most popular feature in the city. She also decided on the most accessible time – midday or perhaps more romantically midnight. Bob might also realise that all was not lost and ask himself what Alice would do. Instead of assuming their date was over before it began, Bob and Alice realised there was a reasonable chance for both to guess a shared solution. They had a fair chance of meeting up at the Eifel Tower.

Alice and Bob were following a strategy described by the Nobel Prize winning American economist Thomas Schelling.[178] Schelling was interested in cold war military strategy and thought it essential to promote cooperation wherever possible. Similarly, Alice and Bob could cooperate without communicating, provided they each knew the other. Alice and Bob both had an internal model of the other's behaviour. They each could predict what the other would do. This is the power of good regulators.

Economics depends on people interacting. John Maynard Keynes introduced a game that modelled the stock market – the Keynesian Beauty Contest. Alice watches a TV contest where people pick the

---

[178] Schelling T. (1990) The Strategy of Conflict, Harvard Univ. Press.

ten most attractive faces from 100 photos. People who chose the most popular faces would get a prize.

If Alice picks the faces she finds most attractive, she might not win. Alice realises this being more sophisticated in her decision-making. She needs to select the ten faces that most people will find good looking. So Alice considers which faces the average person will choose. Alice doesn't stop there, as she now realises others will be trying to pick the most popular faces rather than their own preferences. So Alice ponders what others will decide that others will think the average person will choose. And so on and so forth. Alice is modelling what others will do; she has a theory-of-mind.

Keynes used his beauty contest as an analogy to how people invest in the stock market. It may not be the best short-term strategy to trade based on stock value alone. A stock goes up because traders think the price will rise, and they might make a quick buck. Traders will be asking themselves what other traders will do, trying to predict their behaviour. And round and round we go in a Keynesian beauty contest. Successful traders have an idea of what stocks are popular and why. Like Alice, they have a theory-of-mind.

## Memory

Press and Dyson investigated games where both players only remember the previous move. In many games, such as bridge or chess, a longer memory player has an advantage. Recalling all the earlier cards or multiple chess openings provides a clear advantage. However, for some repeated games like the Prisoner's Dilemma, this is not the case.

In these simple games, the shorter memory player determines the strategy. This is just another way of saying the winner's requisite variety is just enough to model the forgetful player's information. For example, if the opponent with the first move knows only one chess opening, that's what they use. Having extra opening information is redundant for dealing with this limited player, as he does not play those moves.

## Alice Plays Prisoner

To follow what is happening, consider a repeated Prisoner's Dilemma game with Alice playing Bob. Alice is sufficiently intelligent to model Bob, who is a less clever evolutionary player. Indeed, by collecting Bob's responses, Alice can build up knowledge of his play. For example, she can estimate the chance of Bob making a particular move. Now Alice cannot set her own score directly but can persuade Bob to help.

How this works is that Alice is playing Extort. Alice understands Bob's play. So she can enforce a payoff beneficial to her as Bob tries to maximise his return. Alice will reward Bob for his cooperation; otherwise, he might defect. Since even a little reward is better than none at all, Bob plays along to get himself a higher score. As an evolutionary player, that's all Bob cares about.

If Alice decides to play fair, she could be using Tit-for-tat. In Tit-for-tat, Bob's score increases when he cooperates, but so does Alice's. Thus, by playing Tit-for-tat, Alice's score will approximate Bob's whatever he decides to play. However, the more cooperative Bob is, the higher the score they both achieve.

## Extortion

Alice's extortionate play illustrates the difference between players with a theory-of-mind and evolutionary players. Suppose Alice understands strategies to extort the outcome, and Bob just considers increasing his own score. Alice can arrange it so Bob can only do better by helping her. There is no advantage to Bob defecting as he would be hurting himself.

However, if Alice tries to extort smart Bob, things can be quite different. For example, when Alice suggests an unfair division, it becomes a variation on the Ultimatum Game.

In the Ultimatum Game, Alice has to share $100 with Bob. She can suggest any split. Playing fair, Alice would offer a 50-50 split. However, she could equally propose Bob has $1 and keep $99 for himself. The twist is whether Bob agrees. When Bob accepts the split, they will share the money as Alice proposed. If Bob disagrees, neither will receive anything. Of course, in a single game, Alice's rational strategy is to offer $1. If Bob is an evolutionary player, he will agree since he would rather gain $1 than nothing at all.

Confusingly for the sociopaths, people have a sense of fairness in the real world.[179] People often accept offers near 50-50 and reject extreme bids such as 70-30 or worse. A theory-of-mind suggests that the person making the offer is bad news and should not be rewarded. This strategy has benefits in repeated games as you can teach the unfair opponent to play fair. The smart strategy depends on how many times the game repeats and how you might influence other players.

Scientists report chimpanzees and bonobos behave rationally in versions of the Ultimatum Game and do not usually reject unfair offers.[180] In other words, sociopaths play like monkeys.[181]

## Two Smart Players

Suppose Alice and Bob both know about extortion strategies. In that case, they can negotiate a result that provides both with a maximum payoff. Defection would give no advantage. While Alice could defect, it wouldn't increase her score, but it would invite Bob's retaliation.

## Alice's Game

For smart Alice, the game is quite different from what a more naive, selfish player grasps. Alice begins her game by deciding what payoff she wants to squeeze from Bob. Then she finds out if Bob has a theory-of-mind or is an evolutionary player. Alice might know Bob's strategy already. On the other hand, she might begin the game with a trial period examining Bob's play.

If Bob is evolutionary, Alice can fix her strategy and go to the beach. Bob will optimise his payoff and, in so doing, will give Alice the reward that she wants.

---

[179] Oosterbeek H. *et al* (2004) Cultural differences in Ultimatum Game experiments, Experimental Economics, 7, 171–188.
[180] Kaiser I. et al (2012) Theft in an Ultimatum Game, Biol. Lett., 8(6), 942-945.
[181] OK, chimps and bonobos are apes – but "monkeys" was more fun.

If Bob also has a theory-of-mind, Alice needs to pay attention. Bob may not evolve his game to benefit both. Then she switches her strategy to playing the Ultimatum Game. Alice needs to determine what level of inequality Bob will accept. In the worst case, Alice might find Bob pushing her into playing a fair game.

## Bob's Game

If Bob is an evolutionary player, Alice is going to win. Without a theory-of-mind, he does not have the capability of responding to Alice's more advanced strategy. Bob's problem illustrates how Alice's increased cognition provides her with an advantage. Bob does not have the variety to match Alice. He is unable to model her behaviour.

If Bob has an awareness of Alice and a theory-of-mind, he has a further option. Instead of cooperating, he can defect and take the hit to punish Alice. Of course, both will suffer, but he needs to convince Alice that he might cooperate for an increased reward.

## Selfish or Smart?

The standard response to Extort was to show it was not an evolutionary stable strategy (ESS). That is, organisms practising a nice strategy could displace a population using Extort.[182,183] Extort players could gradually lose out as they compete with each other lowering their scores.

As explained earlier, the problem with this objection is that Maynard Smith's ESS has no meaning for smart organisms with a theory-of-mind. Decisively, smart organisms are not playing a classic evolutionary game.

Nonetheless, simple winning strategies are not necessarily stable in the long term. As we have seen, Extort has an advantage in winning games with others. However, when playing another Extort player, it does not perform as well. This is because both are trying to force the other to give up a bigger payoff.

[182] Maynard Smith J. Price G.R. (1973) The logic of animal conflict, Nature, 246 (5427), 15–18.
[183] Adami C. Hintze A. (2013) Evolutionary instability of zero-determinant strategies demonstrates that winning is not everything, Nat. Commun., 4, 2193.

One of the restrictions in repeated game tournaments is the absence of communication. This may simplify the software but is unrealistic. Even microorganisms have sensors and can identify predators and food. As we have seen, the difference between a smart swarm and a dumb crowd is communication.

Extorts theory-of-mind was rudimentary. Thus, Extort was a winning strategy but was vulnerable. It was not a complete model of the opponent and so was not a good regulator. A good regulator has a comprehensive model of the opponent's behaviour. As a good regulator, two Extorts would recognise each other and respond accordingly. Two good regulators would immediately cooperate to maximise their payoff. The real advantage of Extort is not the exploitation but the inclusion of a theory-of-mind.

Let us put forward a good regulator player called GoodReg. GoodReg might use a signal such as a pattern of play to identify and cooperate with other GoodRegs. They thus help each other gain a maximum score.

GoodReg starts with a standard strategy when playing others, say Tit-for-tat, to understand its opponent. In other words, it calculates the probability of the opponent's moves and builds a model of its logic. It might do this using a neural network to keep with the biological analogy.

However, if there are several competing species, each has to be recognised and modelled separately. GoodReg is now becoming complicated. Its neural network is gaining in complexity to be able to identify and model several species. It now has a trade-off between performance in the game and energy and complexity.

Like humans, GoodReg developed a superior neural network and became smarter to match its environment. But GoodReg is not the only competitor capable of a theory-of-mind. Some opposition species can also model their opponents; let's call the new species Smarts. So now we have a different competition.

GoodReg and Smarts are engaged in an information war. When they play, each is analysing and modelling the other. The result of this feeling each other out will result in some level of cooperation or competition. It is what we might describe as a Red Queen optimisation – of their brains. In such an environment, cognitively challenged "evolutionary" players will go extinct. Collaboration and communication underpin the smart solution.

Importantly, these games are highly simplified versions of evolutionary competition. A good regulator does more than model competitors. It models the environment. It can select the most favourable niche, move where its food is abundant, and choose the most suitable mate. Thus, more realistic evolutionary game theory promotes and involves intelligent organisms.

"There will be a layer in the fossil record where you'll know people were here because of the squashed remains of automobiles. It will be a very thin layer".

Lynn Margulis

146

# Consequences

"The road will be rough, but if we are smart enough life will continue on Earth in some form far into the future".

James Lovelock

An application of evolutionary theory drove the eugenics movement. This aspect of social Darwinism, where a group sees themselves as powerful and worthy while others are weak, is usually swept under the carpet. The wealthy and poor are justified by their inferred merit rather than chance and where they were born. Racism, imperialism, and tyranny are also consequences of this view. More critically, people vote for charismatic, strong leaders, and a politician's job description is malignant narcissism.[184] The ultimate result is cycles of political repression and war.

The presence of such people in power leads to organisations behaving for their selfish ends. Indeed, the preeminent requirement for an executive is ruthlessly to increase the profitability of the organisation. Naturally, given the personality types selected, this often takes second place to personal enrichment and aggrandisement. Thus, drug companies put profits before patients, agro-companies put profits before nutrition, universities put profits before students, and weapons companies put profits before peace. It is what many know, but few dare state. Psychopathy, narcissism, and sociopathy underlie the critical problems facing mankind.

Rampant evolutionary biologists pushing a selfish interpretation provide those in power with a justification for this nonsense. A scientist's expected role was to study life rather than develop a psychopathic belief system. As if a minor selection process explains all life on earth! Genetic algorithms are not that powerful and simply do not have the needed properties. Selfish gene stories are not a replacement for the scientific method.

---

[184] Lobaczewski A.M. Knight-Jadczyk L. (2012) Political Ponerology, Red Pill Press.

## Human Exceptionalism

The idea that humans are somehow superior to other organisms leads to the destruction of the environment. We are in another great extinction where biodiversity is crashing as species go extinct.[185] The Holocene or sixth great extinction is underway, driven by humans.[186] Politicians pay lip service to the real issues using the challenge to increase tax or appeal to a green agenda. The problem is human behaviour. Humans are behaving as a parasitoid species over the whole planet and destroying everything in their path. They view other organisms in terms of their utility to themselves. Even a biologist wishing to study microbial ecology might feel it necessary to make a case for the benefit to humans the research will achieve.

Humans may have remarkable brains. They may or may not be massively more intelligent than other creatures, as they claim. What is certain is they are Johnny-come-lately dunces in biological terms. They are actively destroying their own species by psychopathically extreme predation on the planet. When humans have destroyed themselves and many other large creatures, life on earth will likely continue. Microorganisms will hardly have registered the age of humans, and some insects will continue to do well. According to some, these organisms are dumb. But they have survived far longer than the geological blink of an eye that humans have existed. Large brains or not, humans are stupid.

As we have seen, doctors considering themselves to be much more intelligent than microorganisms wasted the antibiotics. They failed to realise these so-called lower organisms had discovered and developed the medical breakthrough millions of years earlier. Medicine merely found what fungi and microorganisms had been using to protect themselves. With a few minor changes, doctors could use these antibiotics in treatment. Doctors failed to see the risks of adaptation and resistance that the microorganisms easily managed. Almost immediately, agriculture started using antibiotics not only for animal health but also as a growth inducer.

---

[185] Ripple W.J. *et al* (2017) World scientists warning to humanity, BioSci., 67 (12), 1026–1028.
[186] Ceballos G. Ehrlich P.R. (2018) The misunderstood sixth mass extinction, Science, 360(6393), 1080-1081.

The result is we now have a plurality of antibiotic-resistant organisms wiping out the medical gains. Doctors appear to be unable to adapt to the developing situation. People may soon be dying in large numbers from infections and avoiding hospitals again. Even when provided with a solution, humans are too irresponsible not to waste it.

There is more to dealing with infections than antibiotics. The failure of medicine is a symptom of a larger malaise. Assuming that the infectious agent is dumb does not work. It means that doctors are forever playing catch up, not realising that they have been outsmarted.

## Barbara McClintock

In her Nobel Prize lecture, Barbara McClintock described how cells respond to shocks with adaptive behaviour. She used the heat shock responses in eukaryotic cells and the bacterial SOS response in bacteria. The cell responds with behaviour that tries to minimise the disturbance, similar to Ross Ashby's homeostat. The cell senses the shock allowing it to adapt. McClintock suggested that genomes could also respond, but the controls are not as adequate. She indicated that genomes could reorganise in response to a shock that threatened the cells survival.

Working with Maize, she found a break in a chromosome produced an extraordinary response. The cells took intelligent action to repair the damage. A cell activated several jumping genes, making anything from minor changes to significant revisions of whole chromosomes. In her words, "They make wise decisions and act on them".

McClintock described cells responding by activating jumping genes (transposons). Jumping genes, as the name suggests, can move position to control an adjacent gene. Some biologists had considered McClintock's suggestion that genes could move about in the chromosomes to be quite mad. However, McClintock realised that stress could initiate cell programs that produce genetic change.

McClintock suggested that these modifications could be the stimulus for generating new species. She explained that we should understand that the genome is part of cell monitoring and

149

responding to shocks. In her words, "We know nothing, however, about how the cell senses danger and instigates responses to it that often are truly remarkable".

McClintock suggested, "A goal for the future would be to determine the extent of knowledge the cell has of itself, and how it utilizes this knowledge in a 'thoughtful' manner when challenged".

## Machine Intelligence

When you allow for the possibility that organisms have a degree of machine intelligence, life becomes even more amazing. Animals are not some dumb meat machines programmed by their DNA. With smart biology, the necessity for a holistic approach extending dull reductionism makes biology exciting again.

The complexity of flowers and their communication with insects is no longer a mystery but an essential outcome of smart organisms interacting with each other. The beauty of the flower is not there to please the aesthetic sense of humans. The pretty petals, fragrances, and nectar are to attract insects, insects with preferences. Logic, learning, and communication act together to produce a wonderful cooperative synergy.

There is a slippery slope. If you allow organisms to have limited smart controls, it rapidly means accepting some are Turing complete. A computer needs very few instructions to be complete. In this context, complete means equal to any other organism. On the other hand, if organisms were not so smart, evolutionary pressure could increase the organisms processing power over time.

Ashby's Laws of cybernetics told us that an organism needs sufficient variety to match and model its environment. Without this ability, the organism would be what Darwin described as unfit and liable to extinction. Thus, an evolutionary driver is pushing for organisms to be sufficiently intelligent to survive. As Ashby suggested, cognition evolves to match the environment.

Some organisms, such as bacteria, are simple, small, and live by being frugal and efficient. An individual microorganism rejects any unnecessary components to be as thrifty as possible. This simplicity should not be taken as an indicator of limited cognition. These organisms can cooperate in swarm intelligence, where simple

150

interactions can be Turing complete once again. We don't recognise bacterial intelligence because it's unfamiliar to us. It works using chemicals and alien time scales.

Machine intelligence can evolve. I gave the example of my efforts using genetic algorithms to generate neural networks. The introduction of game theory into the modern synthesis underscored cognition and purpose. However, limiting the evolutionary discussion to single games emphasised ruthless self-interest while denigrating cooperation and symbiosis. Biologists started explaining altruism as a form of selfish behaviour – apparently, white is also black!

When game theorists included repeated games, nice strategies were superior. Cooperation could beat the coldblooded competition. Ruthless self-interest became a lousy strategy unless modified by cooperation. By contrast, altruism was an excellent strategy, provided it was tempered with retribution. Then Press and Dyson showed that a program with a theory-of-mind could have a winning advantage. They had rediscovered Ashby and Conant's good regulator.

Ross Ashby and Conant explained how the organism must have an internal model of its environment. This is more than a basic theory-of-mind but includes modelling all the variety needed to survive. Without this ability, an organism cannot respond to evolutionary challenges. As a result, the evolution of intelligent organisms is qualitatively different.

## Implications

Putting antibiotics to one side, medicine's primary approach to infection is vaccination. Here they piggyback on the immune system with a technology introduced by Jenner over 200 years ago. The main change over that time has been to understand the organism and its molecular structure more fully. However, these technological improvements to vaccination are minor. Instead, it is the immune system that protects keeping the person safe using biocomputing. The immune system does this by matching the variety of the infecting organisms, antibody to antigen. Indeed, biology is inspirational, and artificial immune systems are an approach to AI and machine intelligence.

Medicine has made less progress with cancer than infectious diseases. Cancer is often treated by removing the lump or with an unintelligent battering of the abnormal cells with radiation or chemotherapy in an attempt to kill them. The idea is to exterminate the cancer. Unfortunately, chemotherapy is a poison given to the patient, as the cancer cells are slightly more susceptible than normal cells. This means that healthy cells are poisoned, and many cancer cells survive. The result is the modern image of a cancer patient as bald and sick.

Let's put the idea of chemotherapy and radiation into a biological context. The cancer drug is a biocide; it kills cells. Farmers use similar biocides called pesticides. They use pesticides locally to reduce the number of insects on a field crop. When farmers limit the application and do not use pesticides too widely, they will be moderately effective. Trying to exterminate the pest is counterproductive. Using pesticides too liberally will rapidly generate resistant insects. In a similar process to antibiotic resistance, the insects adapt, and the pesticide becomes useless.

An entirely similar process occurs with cancer treatments, but the development of resistance is much faster. With chemotherapy, there are billions of cancer cells, and some are shielded from the drug. A typical solid cancer of the breast will contain massively variable cells. That is, each cancer cell could be unique. Cancer cells may have less than 10 or more than 100 damaged and variable chromosomes. A typical healthy body cell will have 23 pairs, no more and no less. In other words, cancer has a massive genetic variety.

Attacking cancer with cytotoxic chemotherapy is generally dumb. Some cancer cells will be highly susceptible to the cytotoxic drug, while others will be highly resistant. The drug kills the sensitive cells leaving the tough cells to grow faster with less competition. The remaining cells are not only immune to the drug but are generally resistant to related treatments.

The development of resistance in cancer is fast because of the vast number of varied cells involved. A small tumour about the size of a sugar cube could contain a billion cells. So it is hardly a surprise that the response to chemotherapy is ultra-rapid drug resistance.

Moreover, the resistance is not specific to the drug. Chemotherapy is a way of making tumours untreatable by any method.

Smart biology provides a new view. Cancer is an adaptive organism, or more precisely, an ecosystem of variable cells. The cells are smart and self-interested, while normal cells are cooperative. Unfortunately, cancer cells are damaged having lost much of their capacity for cooperation. When I describe cancer as selfish cells, it means precisely that. The cells have become selfish. Not abstractly and indirectly as the wishy-washy descriptions of the selfish gene, but explicitly and actively selfish. Their control system or cognition, if you will, has gone awry.

Cancer cells have returned to their biological imperative: trying to survive and reproduce. Short of surgical removal, any attempt to kill cancer will be met with an adaptive response. Ashby's Laws apply. The treatment needs to match the variety in the tumour. Moreover, the intelligence of the physician needs to match that of the cancer. Throwing nasty chemicals or radiation at it is as dumb as believing you can use antibiotics or pesticides with abandon.

## Humility

Instead of glorifying their big brains, perhaps humans need to step back and reassess their progress. One of the leading proponents of Gaia, James Lovelock, has searched for solutions to humanity's impending crisis. His thoughts are that humans will be fortunate to survive the imminent challenges of the current century. I agree.

Lovelock is now 101 years old and considers the current effort the save the planet is hubris. He suggests that the current geological period, the Anthropocene, is nearing the end. The Anthropocene, when humans have affected the environment on a global scale, is only about 300 years old. Lovelock suggests a new era the Novacene is about to begin. He proposes that the Novacene will emerge as AI systems take control. A new dominant species of Cyborgs will populate the planet.

Lovelock's suggests the Cyborgs will have computers many times faster than human brains, and they might consider us as we think of plants. Too slow thinking with incredibly sluggish behaviour. Lovelock is less concerned about terminator machines than I am. I suggest using AI and robotics in war to be a catastrophe for humans just starting to happen. The sociopaths and their followers have a profound tendency to convert every technology into a weapon.

In his optimistic way, Lovelock thinks the Cyborgs will be altruistic. Lovelock's Cyborgs will be hyper-intelligent machines that will need a functioning planet as we humans do. They will also realise they need Gaia for a healthy world. He contrasts this with humans; the currently dominant large species does not look after the planet even though it is essential for their future

By now, the reader may be in a position to consider Lovelock's Cyborgs more realistically. Faster computers are not more intelligent. They are simply faster, performing the same calculations in a shorter time. Speed of cognition may help an individual's short-term survival. Still, slower organisms can match it over time or by swarm intelligence. More memory helps by giving a greater capacity to match the variety in the real world. The primary consideration is the software.

If their software is up to the job of Darwinian survival, the Cyborgs might win in the short term. They are faster and, in principle, can model the behaviour of their human competitors. Let us assume they can work out how to self-reproduce, which requires a fantastic logistics system and the ability to turn raw material into machines. Even if this were achieved, there is still a critical issue. Cyborgs need energy. We are running out of energy and essential commodities. Contrary to popular belief, humans are almost totally dependent on organic fuels. There currently seems no way around this predicament.

We get energy for living by eating other organisms. Historically we started our technological period with fire for heating and cooking. This propelled us from the Stone Age through the Bronze and Iron Ages. We learned how to use coal, and the industrial revolution happened. Each development was based on a new, denser energy source. In no case have we been able to replace a condensed with a less dense energy source. Nuclear replaces oil replaces coal replaces wood.

Modern society is primarily dependent on diesel fuel. A kilo of food bought from a supermarket may cost 10 kilos of oil to produce.

154

Assume it is vegetable as meat is even more energy-intensive. The ground is ploughed using a diesel tractor. The seed is planted using more diesel and sprayed with chemicals obtained from oil. Eventually, the crop is harvested (more diesel). Transported from the farm to the local warehouse (more diesel). It is trucked to the local port (diesel). Placed on a ship (diesel). Transported halfway around the world (diesel). Taken off the ship and trucked to a warehouse (diesel). From the warehouse, it is moved to the factory (diesel). In the factory, it is processed and placed into plastic packages (oil). Then it is trucked to the warehouse (diesel) and on to the supermarket (more diesel). The customer travels to the supermarket in their car and cooks the food using natural gas. As a sustainable system, it is nuts.

Technology does not replace energy. It depends on it. Some people think that changing to electric vehicles will help, but a close examination shows it doesn't work. Each component of the car requires energy. The metal is largely produced using coal, and practical alternatives are absent. There are insufficient rare earth elements for the batteries required. The paint, the tyres, the plastic in the vehicle and so on are dependent on oil. Electricity has to be produced. There is not enough sunlight and wind to replace fossil fuels at current energy usage. Electrical power stations are oil, gas, coal, and nuclear. Nuclear power comes from a power station built using oil, and its uranium fuel is obtained using oil.

Lovelock's Novacene idea fails because technology requires energy that appears to be running out on a global scale. Like improvements in technology, the recent increase in the human population closely follows the widespread availability of abundant energy. Unless we solve nuclear fusion, it seems that our population will soon decline back to pre-industrial levels. The energy problem applies even more to Lovelock's Cyborgs and makes their takeover unlikely.

Human society is at a point of transition. What the future holds is unknowable. An irrational belief in competitive self-interest has failed. Unfettered self-interest may indeed take us to a new and tougher world, red in tooth and claw. Perhaps we should be smart and put more emphasis on things like altruism and cooperation.

155

What a piece of work is a man! How noble in reason, how infinite in faculty! In form and moving how express and admirable! In action how like an angel, in apprehension how like a god!

Hamlet, Act 2, Scene 2, William Shakespeare.

www.ingramcontent.com/pod-product-compliance
Lightning Source LLC
LaVergne TN
LVHW051241050326
832903LV00028B/2509